# THE JUST WAR

# THE
# JUST WAR

*An American Reflection on the*
*Morality of War in Our Time*

## Peter S. Temes

IVAN R. DEE

*Chicago 2003*

Library of Congress Cataloging-in-Publication Data:
Temes, Peter S., 1966–
    The Just War : an American reflection on the morality of war in our
time / Peter S. Temes.
        p.  cm.
    Includes index.
    ISBN 1-56663-534-9 (alk. paper)
    1. Just war doctrine. 2. War—Moral and ethical aspects. I. Title.

U22.T46 2003
172'.42—dc21                                                    2003051507

*This book is part of a general effort to live my life with some connection to the things that matter most. My partner in that project, Judy Temes, matters most of all, and I dedicate this book to her, and to our children Katie, Leah, and Joseph, each a profound companion in our collective journey.*

# PREFACE

I CAN EASILY REMEMBER the moment when Just War philosophy entered my life. I was ten or eleven years old. It was a Friday night, the one night every week my family sat together for a long, somewhat formal dinner to mark the coming of the Jewish Sabbath. We followed none of the religious rules of Sabbath conduct, and we did not go to synagogue, but we did have that dinner every week. While my family ate together in Brooklyn, our nation was taking its final, exhausted steps in its long march through, and now out of, Vietnam. Without any prompting I can remember, I turned to my father and asked him whether he would have fought in the Second World War. "I was too young at the time, but I'd like to think I would have volunteered," he said. Then I asked him whether he would have fought in Vietnam. "I was too old, but I'd like to think I would have refused." It strikes me now, decades later, that I did not ask in reply to either of his answers, why.

Years after that dinner I found myself teaching courses at Harvard University under the general headings "Writing About History" and "Writing About Social and Ethical Issues." In an attempt to understand the ugliness then beginning in the former Yugoslavia, and in a frustrated attempt to *do something* about it, I began teaching a course called "Moral Principles of

War." Only once did a student ask the question the course title begged: Why presume there are moral principles of war to begin with? That's a fine question. Many say that war is what happens when moral principles collapse or are abandoned. But in my life I understood that some things might be rightly fought over, or at least protected with force. The images of the American slave, the Jew in Auschwitz, and the flattened cities of Hiroshima, Nagasaki, and Dresden, their civilian populations killed and exiled, all came to mind. These are all complicated images, to be sure, and they do not fall neatly into the columns of history's anointed and history's despised. Images of Vietnam came to mind too. Vietnam had been the war of my childhood and still a touchstone of youth culture in the pre-Reagan years during which I learned to think about the world beyond America.

The closest I had been to war was a visit to Israel when I was thirteen. While my family and I were visiting a kibbutz in the Upper Galilee, it was shelled from Lebanon. Someone in the nearby town of Kiryat Shmona was hurt or killed, we were told. There would be a response, a counterattack, by the Israel Defense Forces—to what end we never learned.

While teaching about the moral principles of war at Harvard, I enjoyed warm colleagues who had been career soldiers, Pat Hoy most notable among them. A West Point graduate, Pat had been an artillery commander in Vietnam, had returned home to take a Ph.D. in English literature, and had recently retired as the head of the writing program at the U.S. Military Academy with the rank of full colonel. I also came to know a number of military intellectuals who frequented the academic conferences on war and leadership that I began to attend. Howard Prince, the founding dean of the Jepson School of Leadership Studies at the University of Richmond, and himself a recent retiree of

PREFACE

West Point at the time, was among them. Howard had been an infantry commander in Vietnam and had retired as chairman of the department of leadership and psychology at the Military Academy, as a brigadier general. He told me a story about his experience as a fellow at a distinguished European university in the years just before the American involvement in Vietnam escalated dramatically and became, beyond question, a war. Among the many conversations that Prince and his colleagues had about human behavior and world affairs, some inevitably turned toward American intentions in Southeast Asia. And inevitably some formidable young scholar would demand that Prince confess that American motives were no better than those of the French: empire, trade, and glory. No, Prince would say, and then he would explain in patient and reasoned fashion the American philosophy of anti-communism, the Domino Theory, and the collective concern for the good of the world shared by American policymakers. "They were always sure I was lying," he told me, "when in fact I was merely dead wrong."

It had never occurred to me that many—perhaps even most—of the men who had orchestrated and executed the war in Vietnam were more like the thoroughly decent and remarkably brave and able young officer that Howard Prince had been, than like the worst caricatures of Presidents Johnson, Nixon, and their least palatable functionaries of war.

Thus, like many of my generation, I came to the formal study of Just War theory as a skeptic, not seeking guidance, not taking for granted the good intentions of the moral elements of Just War thinking, but coming over time to see in that project something vital. At their worst, Just War principles justify wars that will be waged for their own reasons. At its best, Just War thinking holds back the sword. And in the many instances in between, Just War principles can exert an influence that makes necessary wars briefer and less horrific than they might otherwise be.

Although I and many others have come to Just War theory as skeptics, and many others have come to it through the study of religion, statecraft, or philosophy, more people undoubtedly arrive at it the hard way, through personal experience that leads one to ask—to plead—How can this be just? I saw my own daughters encounter the essence of Just War thinking when they took in with a glance three photographs on the front page of the *New York Times*, depicting a Palestinian father's efforts to shield his son from gunfire. The story of the boy's death and his father's grief was vividly told in those three images, and my daughters were horrified. "Oh, my God," they both said, "how could that happen? That is so wrong." Thirteen and ten, they had their first encounters with Just War thinking. A year later they came home from school early, not knowing exactly why the adult world had been thrown into panic. A longer and deeper engagement with Just War thinking began on that day, September 11.

This book is about Just War theory, but it is not an academic book. In some ways it is a walking tour of the history of Just War ideas. In other ways it is a personal meditation, an effort to connect the core ideas of Just War thinking to the world we live in today. In some ways it is also a personal response to September 11. I began to think seriously about Just War philosophy as the war in Bosnia became a moral preoccupation. Now that the United States has made war on Iraq, and has engaged in something our leaders call a "war" against terror—though with vague enough language that it seems to be a war against certain ideas rather than against a distinct fighting force—Just War thinking is a personal preoccupation once again, and the desire of others to participate in the Just War conversation has once again blossomed like a flower that grows only in proximity to horror.

To a degree, this book is also an exploration of religious ideas about war. Just War thinking in the West begins as a self-conscious endeavor with the Catholic church, building on the inheritance of the Hebrew Bible. And since September 11 we have had no shortage of commentary on traditional Muslim ideas about war—some insightful, some misinformed, and some clearly willful in their hostility and ignorance. This book pays particular attention to the history of ideas about war and civic governance in Islam, and draws connections to the larger project of Just War thinking.

I have tried to rely on secondary sources only minimally, particularly when dealing with the ancient texts. A bit of commentary from professors and scholars does appear in these pages, but this is not a scholarly book and is not meant to encompass any of the ongoing academic debates about the history of Just War theory. It is, rather, a book about ideas and the important meaning those ideas have for us today. Toward that end, as often as possible I have tried to present other people's ideas about Just War clearly and in their original expression.

On a final note, readers will see that the phrase "Just War" is attached to a number of follow-on expressions in this book— Just War thinking, Just War philosophy, Just War theory, and Just War doctrine most common among them. Just War thinking is the phrase I use for the good-faith effort to comprehend the fundamental questions of right and wrong in matters of war. Just War philosophy is the more systematic, and generally more complex, tradition of thought about these questions, and includes the efforts of the great philosophers who have taken them up. Just War theory is the codification of the conclusions that many of these philosophers have arrived at on questions of Just War thinking. Just War doctrine refers to the formal doctrine of the Catholic church relating to war. Although Just War theory is the most commonly used phrase in academic writing about Just War ideas, in most cases I prefer to use Just War thinking and Just War philosophy, precisely because my effort here is to engage in the kind of moral thinking about war that will make sense outside of the academy (with some hope that it will make sense to academics too).

P. S. T.

*Fairfield, Connecticut*
*June 2003*

# ACKNOWLEDGMENTS

THIS BOOK BEGAN with a course I taught as a junior member of the faculty at Harvard University in the early 1990s, when the emerging issue of the day was the war in Bosnia. The late Richard Marius was an important supporter of mine there, a prod and an inspiration. Nancy Sommers allowed me to bend some rules to be able to teach the course. Pat Hoy was an inspiring leader at Harvard and an important source of ideas.

All along Judy Temes has been my chief partner in thinking and talking about these issues. After September 11, 2001, the scholar and sage Sidney Hyman joined me in creating a new version of the Harvard course at the University of Chicago, and became the prevailing spirit of this project.

Sidney's inspiration, contributions, and corrections have been an education in themselves. Ivan Dee has been that rarest of editors and publishers, a thinking man dedicated to the soundness of ideas and language above all else. Irving Rempell remains the origin of my concern with questions of social ethics, and Roberta Lyons and Lloyd Temes the first and best teachers I have had.

# CONTENTS

# THE JUST WAR

# INTRODUCTION:
# THE DUAL NATURE
# OF WAR

WAR IS MESMERIZING. It is front-page news everywhere in the world. It changes everyone touched by it. It combines what we fear most—death, violence, destruction of our homes and communities—with what we love most—courage, loyalty, passion.

To some, war is a self-consuming puzzle: once we answer its riddle, once we understand its causes well enough and become earnest enough in our desire for peace, war will disappear. For others, war is a fundamental fact of life. For all of human history, war seems to have been, and continues to be, one of those things that people do. We eat, we sleep, we make love, we make war.

If there has been any constant quality in the human understanding of war over time, it has been that wars are the ultimate expression of a nation's, and a man's, moral nature. The morality of a nation will be revealed by how and when it fights wars. The morality of a man will be revealed by how and when he fights. Yet the standard poles of morality—good and evil—seem inadequate when we talk about war, or perhaps too adequate: they are the words that leap to mind, but they obscure more than they illuminate about what actually happens in war. These words are too certain; they allow too little room for the moral compromise at the very heart of war—brutal acts for the sake, one hopes, of a good outcome. And so, for the past two thousand years at least, the Western vocabulary for the moral nature of war has revolved around the idea not of the "good" war but of the "just" war, a notion that suggests reluctant duty to do battle and hints at the tactical advantages of having God on one's side.

This dual nature of war is the first complicating factor in any attempt to create, or refresh, a moral approach to war that can play an important role in the policy and practice of war-making in the world today. It is a function of the two forces that make war: individuals and groups (and the phrase "make war" sits here with its ambiguities intentionally on display—*make* as in set war in motion, and *make* as in commit the singular acts of war, individual by individual).

One side of this dual nature is war as the story of the individual soldier pushed to his physical and moral limits. The other side is war as the story of the state, also pushed to its limits. Ancient perspectives on war generally emphasized the individual's struggle; modern ideas about war emphasize the role of the state.

In most tribal cultures, the moral scale of war is small. The clan and the tribe sit in the background. They set the context for war and are the witness to war's shaping and revealing of men's characters; but war itself is mostly a matter of the actions of individuals. The stories told by Wooden Leg, a Northern Cheyenne warrior at the Battle of Little Big Horn, offer a particularly clear example. Wooden Leg claims to have taken part of General Custer's scalp as he lay dead on the battlefield (though unlike many others there that day, he makes no claim to have struck the coup de grace against the general). Wooden Leg describes riding in pursuit of Custer's men at the very moment it dawned on him that he and his fellow Cheyenne and Sioux fighters might actually win their battle against the U.S. Cavalry that day (a rare occurrence). "Our war cries and war songs were mingled with many jeering calls," he told the historian Peter Nabokov, "such as 'You are only boys. You ought not to be fighting.'" Notice that the jeer is personal, directly aimed at the character of the individual warriors—they are not men but children. Wooden Leg continues: "Little Bird and I were after one certain soldier. Little Bird was wearing a trailing war bonnet. He was at the right and I was at the left of the fleeing man. We were lashing him and his horse with our pony whips. It seemed not brave to shoot him." How striking that Wooden Leg describes the soldier he is about to kill as "the fleeing man." That phrase bares the humanity of the soldier and his vulnerability. To a degree it makes him seem frail, but it also restores to him some of the humane and individual character that is diminished by his status as a soldier in his nation's uniform. For both good and ill, Wooden Leg's perspective focuses on the man and not the nation. And, of course, Wooden Leg's emphasis on bravery precisely embodies the tribal idea that battle is about individual character.

This tribal perspective is ancient, predating American Indian cultures by centuries. The oldest surviving narrative, the epic of Gilgamesh, dates from about 2000 B.C. in its earliest rendition, and captures a similar sense of war as the story of individual men. The epic opens with the story of Gilgamesh's adventures as a traveling warrior, moving from town to town for plunder. "Gilgamesh went abroad in the world," the more readable of the widely used translations begins, "but he met with none who could withstand his arms until he came to Uruk. But the men of Uruk muttered in their houses, 'Gilgamesh sounds the tocsin from his amusement, his arrogance knows no bounds. . . .'" Like so many ancient epics, the epic of Gilgamesh tells the story of battle as the story of one man's character. The wars recounted in the epic are expressions of the bad character of Gilgamesh and the response to him of men and gods. Readers familiar with Homer's *Iliad* will recognize the similar structure of both epics' opening lines: a warrior's arrogance sets the stage for tales of fighting, death, and the characters of a few good men.

The more modern sense of war, best captured in the Prussian military thinker Carl von Clausewitz's remark that war is politics by other means (not Clausewitz's exact words but a fair representation of his thinking), brings the state into the center of war's meaning and enlarges the moral scale of war dramatically. War today is generally seen as a theatre of abstractions in conflict: states, civilizations, and even ideas themselves are the central actors. We talk about the American "war against terror" and the "clash of civilizations" at the center of today's most dramatic wars, echoing the First World War's ambition to "make the world safe for democracy." Terror, civilizations, and democracy are remarkably abstract reasons for asking young men and women to put on uniforms, kill, and die.

To understand war today, though, we need to find a balance between these two perspectives, to reconcile this dual nature of war so that we can understand why, when, and with what meaning we make war. This need is on the one hand absolute. Any act of war is an act both of the group *and* of the individual. Striking just the right balance between the two, in the language and ideas surrounding a war, offers a degree of moral clarity (and the tactical advantage that moral clarity carries with it). On the other hand, this balance is critically important specifically for our age, because our technology brings modern and ancient cultures into close and extended contact.

Consider, for example, the prevailing popular image of the events leading to the terrorist assault on New York City in September 2001: men living in nearly prehistoric conditions plot terror from their caves, then move by foot, horse, and donkey hundreds of miles to the nearest paved roads, then into the medieval cities of their world, and then to Hamburg, Rome, New York and California and Florida, and ultimately into the cockpits of the most modern passenger jets, and from there to their deaths, and the deaths of thousands of innocents, broadcast live to hundreds of millions of television watchers around the globe. Or consider a simpler image of the same collage of ancient and modern: in those caves, laptop computers held plans for the attack.

From Gilgamesh to Clausewitz to the First and Second world wars, an evolution from the tribal to the modern seems to take place as the balance of war's meaning shifts from an emphasis on the individual to an emphasis on the state. But this slowly built balance between ancient and modern seems to collapse as ancient cultures and modern cultures come together so freely, so often, and so intensely as they do today.

After centuries in which the fundamental questions of war were about how to fight most effectively, whether for empire or for self-defense, we are left with all the tools for military victory assembled in our modern arsenals but without the intellectual and moral tools for understanding when and why to use them. Just now the West turns with its military powers awakened toward the villages, caves, and refugee camps of the large undeveloped areas of Central Asia and the Middle East—and just as easily, perhaps sooner than we think, toward other still-ancient swaths of the rest of the world. The moral spark, the motive of higher purpose, is at best diminished in modern Western culture's engine of battle because we are, collectively, confused about when and why war is a proper choice, when and why it can be just. Without that spark, all our devices and technologies threaten us every bit as much as they threaten others.

While frightening in some ways and exhilarating in others, the technology-enabled blending of near and far, of ancient and modern, makes it clear that a Just War theory for our own age must be built on a broad platform. We must draw from the thinking about war that we inherit from the distant past, on the modern Western traditions of thought about the strengths and limitations of modern states, and on the rich tradition of religious thought about war. The project of this book is to articulate a moral view of war that accepts the wisdom and moral substance of our tribal origins, is broadened by the modern philosophical notions of war as a conflict of modern states and "world orders," and makes room as well for the rich religious tradition of Just War thinking. From these three principal sources we can form a moral view of war that will help us understand—and perhaps to limit—the modern experience of war.

# 1

# "WE GO TO WAR THAT
# WE MAY HAVE PEACE"

AUGUSTINE, the first clear voice in the Christian tradition that established the primacy of the phrase "Just War," wrote in the fifth century A.D., "We go to war, that we may have peace."* In this phrase, at an early date, he captured the essence of the modern view of war. War for Augustine was not about the experience of the individual, not about the refinement or revelation of man's character, and not a central or essential part of civilization. It was a means to an end. More to the point, Augustine finessed the obvious contradiction between means and ends: he allowed that evil might not be evil if in service to good, that sin might not be sin if in service to grace—a concept that came to

---

*The Roman military figure Vegetius, writing at roughly the same time as Augustine, notably said that "he who desires peace must prepare for war." His meaning was a good deal less subtle than Augustine's, though. The larger work at hand for Vegetius was to prepare a summary of Greek knowledge and technique of war for the emperor, and he took for granted that "peace" was a rough equivalent of "victory."

be known as the idea of "double effect" in the vocabulary of Just War philosophy. Thus Augustine was an early embodiment of the contradictions at the heart of the Catholic church's beginnings in the fourth century, once it became the official religion of the late Roman empire. These contradictions are equally true of any religion that directly exercises the power of government or sits in any sense beside a governor, as a state religion.

Many centuries later, George Orwell applied this contradictory (and quite modern) view of war to the task of national leadership. Orwell wrote, "People sleep peaceably in their beds at night only because rough men stand ready to do violence on their behalf." These words apply equally to the men and women who decide whether, when, and how a nation goes to war as they do to the men and women who fight on the ground (or, in our age, in the air). Where Augustine had said that the purpose of war is peace, now Orwell adds that peace itself is a function of ongoing war or, more precisely, the ongoing *readiness* for war. The best summation of the moral high ground that Augustine and Orwell mark out is that war is always wrong—it always represents a horrible failure to find alternatives—but sometimes necessary. This seems to me the most reasonable and workable moral observation of war in general that also takes into account the social, political, and moral events that surround wars as they occur.

Augustine's job as a churchman prevented him from acknowledging the kernel of moral failure that sat within the larger moral system of Christianity—the *wrong* in "war is always wrong but sometimes necessary"—once the Christian enterprise took up the task of Just War doctrine. Thus his acceptance of the very idea of "Just War" is less reluctant than Orwell's, and at times all too enthusiastic (he goes on to say that for the good

Christian, war is actually a peaceful pursuit). Augustine is as close as we can come to a founder of Just War theory in the Western tradition, and in that role he becomes a symbol of the dark side of Just War thinking: the function of apologist, providing moral cover to those who wish to make war for their own reasons. Writing in the age of the first Christian kings, Augustine essentially invented the theory that allowed those kings—the Roman emperor Constantine was the first—to follow the teachings of Jesus on the one hand, and to kill by the hundreds and thousands on the other. Still, Augustine led mainstream Christian philosophy to a vital point of moral clarity: war is wrong as an end. In the age of the first Christian statesmen, he codified the idea that peace—what Orwell would later characterize as peaceable slumber—is the only proper answer to the ultimate questions of statesmanship and national leadership, and that was quite an innovation for the fifth century.

In theory this goal of statesmanship can be reached by peaceable means, yet no period of human history has yet shown this theory to be true. Thus Augustine's idea that the purpose of war is peace seems plausible in theory though radically incomplete in practice. It is a promise, a reflection on the interior impulses that lead to the exterior acts of war, and in its seeming contradiction it seeks a balance that perhaps limits war, perhaps excuses it. Its value lies in how it is understood by those who seek to adhere to it. The lesson might be, Don't make war unless your goal is peace. Or it might be, War is okay in general, because in general its aim is peace.

Orwell's observation that peace is possible only because of readiness to fight seems more a description of what is than a considered philosophy. Thus Orwell represents an important perspective in the Just War tradition: the realist who does not necessarily see a divine hand in the workings of war, who sees war as a bad thing to be stopped if possible and limited always, but who also has enough practical imagination to understand that the absolute rejection of war means victory for forces that ought, on their merits, to be fought against.

To look at the world today is to see war and the imminent threat of war in the Middle East, in Northern Ireland, in Central Asia and Western Africa, and upon literally hundreds of smaller stages with names like Nagorno Karaback, Kashmir, and San Cristobol de las Casas. What are the decent human being and the decent political state to do? If we begin with the idea that war is wrong and therefore that no man, woman, or state ought to undertake it, we find ourselves in an immediate contradiction: greater and more grievous war in the long run will follow in many of these places if the only response to attacks on the innocent is inaction—even inaction motivated by the highest ideals. Choosing not to raise arms will often result in the arms of others being raised more flagrantly. History is replete with evidence that absolute moral abstinence from war leads in many cases to more war, not less (the British response to Hitler's small wars of the late 1930s is a clear case study, about which more later). And any anti-war strategy that leads to more war is obviously inadequate—it simply does not reach its own objectives.

This book—and the entire enterprise of Just War philosophy—begins only here, after the moral desire for peace instead of war is clear, and then only after the sentimental application of pacifism is seen as a fond dream inadequate to its own ends as a tool of national policy or decisive political thought. This is not to say that pacifism is wrong or that pacifists have a destructive influence. To the contrary, the voice of conscience—the voice that reminds us of the *wrong* in the idea that war is always wrong but sometimes necessary—is vital. But it is vital as a piece of the whole, not as a response complete in itself.

The larger perspective, one that accepts responsibility for outcomes as well as for intentions, leads us to the essential Just War formulation: War is wrong, but we must accept the moral challenge not of life lived in some timeless ideal but of *our* lives in *our* times—not of the possible world but of the world as it is. Thus we discover that a nation must sometimes choose not only between right and wrong but between wrong and wrong. Thus war, always wrong, always a sin, may nevertheless become at times the only decent option. In every case we can trace the moment of war's necessity back to the point at which we see that had *this* choice been made rather than *that* one, had *this* man or woman been given the presidency or the admiralty or the ambassadorship or the payoff, rather than *that* man or woman, the war before us might indeed have been avoided. This kind of observation is always important to the historian, and often to the statesman and the soldier and the citizen, but it is rather useless to those who must decide that *now we fight* or *now we hold our fire*. Indeed we are fools—or worse—to have missed the chance to avoid war, but given the moment we find ourselves in, war may nevertheless be the least worst—indeed, the only—option. Wrong, but necessary.

## THE PEACEFUL PURSUIT?

Thomas Aquinas, in the thirteenth century a significant interpreter of Augustine on war and an important thinker about war in his own right, in his book *Summa Theologica* makes the case that war is never free of sin: "Nothing, except sin, is contrary to an act of virtue. But war is contrary to peace. Therefore war is always a sin." But Aquinas does not say this because he means it. Rather, he presents this simple formulation as an "objection" to his own thesis that war can be just fine under the right circumstances. He quotes Augustine for clarification: "True religion looks upon as peaceful those wars that are waged not for motives of aggrandizement, or cruelty, but with the object of securing peace. . . ." So in some cases war is not really a sin, Augustine and Aquinas say, because if a war meets the criteria of Just War, it is not only the pursuit of peace but also a peaceful pursuit. Recall, though, that both Augustine and Aquinas were talking about war within the larger context of Christianity. The Christian goal of all human behavior was to live humble and good lives, and to go to heaven. The Christian moral system these two men were explaining—and to a degree inventing— was meant to be all encompassing and to offer the good man the opportunity to follow an uncompromised path free of sin.

It is perhaps a bit of philosophical shirking to say that the project of Just War thinking today does not accept the larger systematic challenge of guiding the individual to heaven, but that is indeed the case. In face the project here is to apply moral principles without having to accept larger philosophical or religious systems—that is, to see the wars of our time as clearly as possible and with full advantage of all the available moral perspectives on them, but without prior allegiance to any orthodoxy. Taking up this challenge will never leave us in that benighted state that Augustine and Aquinas would like the Christian warrior to enjoy—the state of the peaceful warrior. Yet accepting the challenge of Just War thinking without the larger Christian system—or the larger Jewish system, or the larger Muslim, Hindu, or Humanist system, or any particular system at all—is precisely what allows us to take up the practical challenge that faces policymakers: not the challenge of what is ultimately right, but the challenge of what is best among the options before us.

Thus we can say that choosing war is choosing the wrong, but there are moments when it is the only decent choice. We are released from the burden of pretending that at times war is not really war. A Just War theory that works tells us how to recognize those moments and how to distinguish them from moments in which peace is a real option and the noblest choice, when Orwell's readiness is itself enough, and Augustine's war for the sake of peace is not—not yet—needed.

## THE STATE AS LEGITIMATE AUTHORITY

In much of the world, the question of whether war can be just begins with the question of who is doing the fighting, not in the sense of who is shooting their guns or raising their swords but in the sense of what kind of organization is organizing the larger enterprise of the war. In fact, Catholic Just War doctrine, which has been the foundation of Just War thinking in the West, asks as its first question, Is this war being led by a legitimate authority?

The word "authority" is ambiguous here: it does not require that a war be the action of a government—in that case the phrase would be "legitimate government." Instead the word "authority" seems to allow for the idea that a Just War might also be undertaken by, as examples, revolutionary movements, breakaway provinces, clans, tribal groups, or religious sects. But Just War thinking became increasingly important in Western history as organized political states came to dominate, and tribes, clans, and other local social structures lost their supremacy. Today wars are fought largely by states, or against them. While many modern wars are the work of ragtag armies of rebels and angry irregulars, these half-organized forces tend to direct their violent efforts against the various faces of the states they live near or within. Even when a war takes the form of revolt today, the revolt is generally about the fact of a state— how bad it is, how unjust, how it must be changed or destroyed. The idea of the state remains the organizing principle.

This applies as well to the organizing principles of Al Qaeda, the international fundamentalist terror group largely financed and led by Osama bin Laden. Bin Laden's first recognized enemy was the Soviet Union as it sought dominance in Afghanistan. Then in 1991 bin Laden agitated for Saudi Arabia, his home nation and the bastion of a backward-looking form of Islam that bin Laden quite liked, to save Kuwait in the name of Islam from massing Iraqi troops. To his horror, bin Laden saw Saudi rulers pass on the chance to fight what would have been, at best, an evenly matched battle, and choose instead to host the far more persuasive American armed forces during what became the Gulf War. In the process, the Saudi state became one of bin Laden's targets while the United States became for him the embodiment of evil and his greatest enemy.

What do the former Soviet Union, Saudi Arabia, and the United States have in common that might motivate bin Laden's forces to see them as an enemy axis? Certainly not religion. We are looking at a militantly atheist imperial power, a profoundly conservative Muslim state, and, arguably, a nominally nonsectarian world power with a mildly Christian bent. The common traits that infuriate bin Laden are the very features of modern statehood, in particular the principles of compromise and collective common interest that form the realpolitik of governance among a large and varied population. And that is exactly what bin Laden opposes. Far better, in his view, was the Taliban state of Afghanistan, a state that could not feed its people, sustain roads, or even support a realistic national identity. Instead, all of Afghanistan took on the character of the disconnected tribal village, with every citizen subject to the whims of the head man or whatever marauding force might come to town and prove even tougher, and subject as well (and with more devastating effects) to weather, disease, and hunger. A modern state centralizes, structures, and codifies power. It recognizes the significance of the individual citizen. It facilitates contact and exchange with the wider world. It draws power away from the local despot and makes the individual's relation to the state as important or more important for civic life as the relationship to the head of the clan, the village, or the church. It diminishes the impact of the local leader's whim and makes the rule of civic law a central virtue. For all these reasons, Al Qaeda hates the United States. Its spasmodic war on the secular West is very much about the modern state, the enemy that gives it form. Thus bin Laden's ideal: a war against the state that culminates in a nominally Muslim nonstate, blind to the well-being of the individual and content in its own collective material decline. The essential qualities of the modern state are bin Laden's enemies; the very idea of the modern state, a specter and a menace. Thus in the world as we find it today, even the wars of the anti-statist are animated by the state, if for no other reason that to fight against it.

## RAGE AND THE TRIBAL VISION OF WAR

But this was not always so. Wars have not always been driven by the will of states or the will to destroy them. The very first word of Robert Fagles's translation of Homer's *Iliad* is "Rage": "Rage—Goddess, sing of Peleus' son Achilles,/murderous doomed, that cost the Achaeans countless losses. . . ." Seven lines later, the *Iliad* continues, "What god drove them to fight with such fury?/ Apollo, son of Zeus and Leto. Incensed at the king/ he swept a fatal plague through the army—men were dying/ and all because Agamemnon spurned Apollo's priest." The story of the *Iliad* is the story of the Trojan War, but it is also—indeed, first and foremost—the story of rage, of one man's anger. And the give-and-take of battle (and the health and well-being of the troops) reflects the active involvement of a god, Apollo. For Homer, war was not so much a matter of states as a matter of the passions of men and gods. The American philosopher William James makes passing reference to the *Iliad* in his essay "The Moral Equivalent of War" (about which more later). He describes the *Iliad* as "one long recital of how Diomedes and Ajax, Sarpedon and Hector killed. No detail of the wounds they made is spared us, and the Greek mind fed upon the story. Greek history is a panorama of jingoism and imperialism—war for war's sake, all the citizens being warriors. It is horrible reading—because of the irrationality of it all—save for the purpose of making 'history'—and the history is that of the utter ruin of a civilization and intellectual respects, perhaps the highest the earth has ever seen." With somewhat modern eyes, James views the personal glories of pervasive battle with disgust, precisely because he is thinking at the level of "civilization" and the state where Homer's *Iliad* tells a story at the level of the individual. James sees the drama of Greek civilization where Homer sees the drama of men's hearts, minds, and bodies. Homer takes for granted what the path-breaking Muslim historian Ibn Khaldun wrote in fourteenth-century Spain, that war is a universal and inevitable aspect of life, ordained by God to the same extent as the sky and the earth, the heat and the cold. The question of *whether* to fight is not a significant moral question because fighting is constant; the minor decision not to fight this war will be made only in the context of knowing that another war will present itself soon enough, because it is simply always there. The significant moral question is rather about the individual's role in the wars that unfold through his life: What kind of warrior is he?

The American Indian practice of "countain coup" reflects a similar sense of war as a personal drama rather than the drama of states in conflict. Among the many practical advantages that Euro-Americans held in their armed conflicts with American Indians was that they functioned as part of a fairly modern state and generally saw their battles with Indians as part of the larger American drama of "opening the frontier," expanding the American nation's physical footprint, wiping out a threat to settlers, and even vanquishing a weaker civilization. American Indian fighters tended to see the fighting differently. For many Indians battle was, as for the early Greeks, a matter of individual men defining themselves and following the spirits of their ancestors. Thus the importance of "counting coup," the American Indian practice of laying a hand on one's enemy in battle before his death, saying one's name and the name of one's father, and then striking the death blow. Imagine an American cavalryman on horseback heading into battle, looking for the opportunity to shoot and kill an Indian warrior at a distance, rifle cocked and ready to fire. Against him stands an Indian, perhaps armed with a rifle, perhaps with a battle knife or lance, looking for the chance to lay hands on the man on horseback before killing him. In practical terms, the advantage is all the cavalryman's— he will kill from a distance in order to bring faster victory to his cavalry unit, his army, and his nation. The Indian warrior hopes to kill in a battle of man against man, expressing the cultural sense that war is a matter of the individual's intention and character, as it was with the Greeks.

Consider the last line of the *Iliad*: "And so the Trojans buried Hector, breaker of horses." Thus the epic story of the Trojan War ends with one man's death. The Trojans—the tribe of the people of Troy—act collectively to bury and memorialize their warrior. The larger idea of "the Trojans" operates more in their grief than in their taking up arms. The arms are the work of one man at a time. Understanding, celebrating, and memorializing the war is, from this perspective, the proper work of the group.

This is as close as we can come to a starting point, a baseline idea, for how people think about war: once we thought about war as the actions of individual men in battle. The clan, the tribe, and the nation hung in the background—they set the context and were witness to war's shaping and revealing of men's character. In this early model there is little view of war being either right or wrong in the larger sense: wars might be fought badly or well, but wars themselves are taken for granted as part of the natural state of things. Even the Trojan War itself, as Homer tells it, is something of a misadventure. Although Homer talks in the opening lines of the *Iliad* of the war's bad cause, the real drama of the war is the collectivity of the acts of men. The very badness of the war's bad cause is not the badness of a state but the badness of one man—one man's rage—compounded by the badness of other men. And so the moral scale of war is small. The beginning proposition of this chapter, that war is always wrong though sometimes necessary, would not make sense in this tribal context. How, after all, could war always be wrong if every man is expected to test himself in war in order to reveal to himself and his community just who he is? War has too vital a social function to play for it to be inherently wrong.

Yet today the idea that war is always wrong but sometimes necessary makes sense. I can remember first hearing that Clausewitz definition—"War is politics by other means"—when I was a graduate student, and being underwhelmed by it. What else could war be? But my perspective was all too modern. Clausewitz was describing a transition that has by now been under way for centuries, a transition to an understanding of war that most twenty-first-century people take for granted as a near-universal norm, accepted by all but terrorists and madmen. I had assumed that war had always been essentially political and obviously centered on the state. I took for granted that war was by its nature an act of state. Clausewitz's challenge, though, began with the old notion of war as, in its essence, the flame that hardened men's bodies and souls, the stage for their personal struggle and initiation. To this premodern sense of war, Clausewitz posed an alternative vision based upon what he had seen in a life of battle against Napoleon's armies. The older, tribal view of war is of course still with us, but now it is the minor chord played against the dominant theme of the modern state as the chief actor in the drama of war.

## WAR AND THE RISE OF THE RIGHTS OF MAN

President Woodrow Wilson addressed Congress on April 2, 1917, as he led the United States into the First World War. "We are glad," he told Congress, "now that we see the facts with no veil of false pretense about them, to fight thus for the ultimate peace of the world and for the liberation of its peoples, the German peoples included: for the rights great and small and the privilege of men everywhere to choose their way of life and of obedience. The world must be made safe for democracy. Its peace must be planted upon the tested foundations of political liberty. We have no selfish ends to serve. We desire no conquest, no dominion. We seek no indemnities for ourselves, no material compensation for the sacrifices we shall freely make. We are but one of the champions of the rights of mankind. We shall be satisfied when those rights have been made as the faith and the freedom of nations can make them." Vividly drawing from the Declaration of Independence, Wilson is about to make war—or at least he says he is about to make war—for the sake of a philosophy. He might prefer to say, for *the* philosophy, the philosophy of freedom. Be that as it may, these are astoundingly abstract principles for which to send one's children off to fight and die. Wilson knows this, in particular when he says, "We have no selfish ends to serve. We desire no conquest, no dominion." The Declaration of Independence, the fundamental document in making the case for war based on philosophical principles, was a remarkable balance of the universal ("all men are created equal") with the local (King George had "made Judges dependent on his Will alone, for the tenure of their offices and the amount and payment of their salaries"). Yet Wilson does not speak of practical interests at all. Instead he speaks entirely of the universal. He does not speak of the experience of individuals; instead he speaks of the experience of all humanity. His rhetoric is extreme—he leaps to the level of war as the act of states, and then goes beyond, to war as the act of all humanity.

Wilson's position was similar to that of President George W. Bush as he contemplated—indeed, campaigned for—war with Iraq in 2002. Bush made the argument not of self-interest, not even of national interest, but of moral absolutes. Saddam must go, he said more than once, because he is evil. This is a powerful statement, and it speaks directly to the moral calculus of war. But just as the absolute pacifist is deaf to the significance of Augustine's first principle, that the goal of war is peace, so is the moralist-at-arms blind to the prospect of eternal bloodshed in pursuit of God's grace. After Saddam, who else among the evil shall we fight? The armed moralist sees no end of war, just as he sees no end of evil.*

Compare the idea of making the world safe for democracy to the motives we find in classical literature about war—motives like plunder and empire on the one hand, and personal honor and ethnic hatred on the other—and we can see the change in both the scale of justification, from the local to the global, and the degree of abstraction, from the personal (honor) and practical (plunder) to the entirely philosophical. These distinctions

---

*The theologian Reinhold Niebuhr is perhaps the most striking example of the armed moralist. In the 1950s he argued that Christian morality demanded that the Soviet Union be condemned. Once condemned, and in the name of the innocent millions living under Communist dictatorship, regime change was not only justified but mandatory; any moral nation with the ability to ensure swift and absolute victory was obligated to strike with its full might. Ergo, this professor of Christian ethics argued, the obligation for an American nuclear first strike against the Soviet Union.

can matter little—to be killed in the name of democracy is not very different from being killed in the name of empire—or they can matter a great deal. We may question whether we are true to our goals as we make war (did the United States resist the impulse to take conquest and dominion in the First World War?). We may also ask whether those goals are, first, worth fighting for (George W. Bush's return to the fact that Saddam is a leader who "gasses his own people" creates a clear motive—to aid those whom Saddam would destroy), and, second, possible (to vanquish evil is an ambition so extreme and superhuman that it seems to fall of its own weight as a justification of war).

Tribal motives for war, centered on the individual more than on the group, invite less reflection and encourage less debate. They build on the local and the personal, emphasizing the experience of the individual, first, and the home community second and last. The tribal perspective celebrates the warrior spirit and looks deeply into the experience of war, but its moral scale is small: it is the experience of a dynamic individual in a static world. It is the narrowness of vision that leads to Americans calling the time of our war in Southeast Asia "Vietnam," as though there were no nation—in this case a nation with a two-thousand-year history—of that name. It is the inward-looking memory that answers the question "How many were killed in the American war in Vietnam?" with a number close to fifty thousand, the number of American soldiers killed, when most estimates of the number of Vietnamese combatants killed begin at one million.

The more modern alternative to this constricted view—an alternative not only to what came long ago but also to the narrower moral impulses we can easily find in modern thought and talk about war—is, to a degree, the legacy of Augustine's notion that the ultimate purpose of war is peace. It is the modern view of war that begins to dominate the thinking of civil and military leaders around the time of the great revolutions in America and France, and it finds clear expression in the work of the idealists Kant and Rousseau, the philosopher of history Hegel, and the man of war who wrote so clearly about it, Clausewitz. But why did this legacy begin to reassert itself so forcefully in the eighteenth century?

Some scholars answer this question by pointing to the history of Christian ethics. They see an evolution that reaches a natural point of influence at about that time, building on the platform laid by Thomas Aquinas in particular. But something larger was happening in Europe at about this time, not entirely apart from Christian ethics and church history but owing more to the advent of sailing ships that could cross oceans, and to the revolution in secular thinking that the spiritual ideas of Immanuel Kant represented.

In the late 1700s, just as the modern nation-state was emerging in Europe, Kant argued that all human life is equally precious. His idealism demands a recognition that killing is never only the story of the killer but also of the killed. If a hundred men die in a battlefield rout, Kant's modern sensibility recognizes tragedy as well as victory on that battlefield. It demands that whoever considers that battle ask why the lives were lost. It rules out satisfaction with the tribal notion that war is simply thus, that men will always die in battle. Kant's entire philosophy centers on the imagination of the individual and the capacity of each individual to make sense of moral principles without needing to cede moral judgment to external authorities. Rather than accept the presumption that war is the normal state of things, Kant's notion of the individual's responsibility to understand what transpires around him pushes the individual to ask what a death in battle accomplishes, beyond whether the soldier now dead has died well. Kant's emphasis on individual reasoning is a direct product of his belief that all human life is equally precious. With this in mind, we must ask what more precious end is served by every death in war. And we must ask in each cast whether there is a better way to reach the same ends. These questions—emphasizing alternatives, and resting on the experience of the individual—are a large measure of what it means to be modern, at least in the ways we think about war.

The era of the great revolutions brought with it the emergence of the idea of individualism and of the idea that government may change—and wars may be fought—not merely for the sake of power but for the sake of individual rights. Questions of the purpose and function of nations began to be reframed and answered in new ways. States began to be seen as deriving their legitimacy from the bottom up rather than from the top down. Simultaneously, war began to be seen more distinctly as an enterprise of the state, not necessarily of man, whether king or soldier. New kinds of states and new kinds of legitimacy for the state fostered a migration of meaning, turning what had once been a test of men into a test of the state. As an advocate for the individual, with its legitimacy resting on its service to the individual, the state absorbed the kind of moral duty that had earlier been masked by an expectation that a state had best be strong, perhaps benevolent, but hardly supplicant. Recall Plato's *Republic*: the good state is the good man writ large; virtue is in control and order, the balancing of the worst impulses with the better. With the Enlightenment, virtue in the ideal state becomes more a matter of service than control. The question, Does this state keep its people under control?, is replaced by the question, Does this state serve its people well? And so in war, the moral burden of the individual falls to the state.

Consider the question of how states fail. Gibbon offered the model of Rome falling because it catered to the weaknesses of its citizens and offered too little control of their worst impulses. The moral question here was, How well does the state regulate its citizens? But Augustine set in motion a different kind of question about the state: How well does it draw its citizens to do good for others? The medieval Christian interpretation of this question, alas, was a Crusader's inquiry: How can we save the souls of heathens or, failing that, vanquish them? But in the age of the Enlightenment, the state bears a new kind of moral burden: How can a state prove to be of good character by strengthening and serving the inherent rights of men, both its own citizens and all men generally? War comes to be seen through a similar prism: How does war serve the rights of man? How does war further the exercise of what is universally good rather than what is good for one man, one tribe, or one nation? Thus the shift from the tribal to the modern is in part a shift from the parochial to the universal. War moves from being the story of a man to being the story of all men, of the collective spark of divinity within every man.

Of course this shift to an Enlightenment sense of the rights of man is hardly an accomplished fact, even today. Many would argue that even the United States and France have barely begun to live up to the ideals that were forcefully articulated and em-braced in their declarations and revolutions. The evolution from war as the story of a man to war as the story of all men is at best in some midpoint, at worst only one ideal among many that have enjoyed their vogue and passed on unfulfilled. But the image of armies fighting for an ideal, on behalf of states organized as tools for advancing the rights of men, is a compelling alternative to the image of tribal conflict. Without question, the emergence in the 1700s and 1800s of a new idea about the purposes of the state and how it gains legitimacy is at the root of the new ideas about war that emerge at roughly the same time.

War becomes a principal way that states move from the old, discredited idea of divine right and conscripted citizenry to the new and better idea of the state as the servant of the rights of man. War becomes an essential part of the story of the evolution of the idea of the state, as strong and compelling a story as that of any one man under arms. The new idea of the state makes war the story of the state just as the state itself becomes much more dynamic, much more critical and open to the flux of ideas and desires of its people. This new state elevates the individual mightily. And so war shifts its center toward the state, just as the state shifts its center toward the individual.

This newly balanced view of war sees the moral substance of the individual as an actor in war. The moral substance of the state is also an actor—and creator—of war, often waged in the name of the collective interests of the individual. We must see with the moral vision that in tribal individualism demands the honor of the warrior (an idea similar to the Christian notion of *jus in bello*, just conduct in war) and in modern times demands decency among the nations, rebels, breakaway regions, and self-styled armies of liberation that make war (*just ad bellum*, just policy in when and where to make war). If we do not, we too easily become guilty of the ancient sin of sanctifying the honorable warrior who builds victory for evil, and of the modern sin of ignoring the evil that some men do even when they serve in the armies of freedom.

Yet the twining together of the individual and the group aspects of war remains an exercise in moral contradiction. It embraces the notion that war not only can be won but can even be in some sense a glorious success. It also embraces the notion that war is always a tragedy and always a failure. In fact both ideas seem true. Most wars do indeed leave a winner standing, a nation or a group of people who have met at least some of their objectives in battle and have left their enemy weakened to the point of surrender or retreat. That is victory of a sort. And the characters of men, as well as the characters of nations, are not only revealed but changed by war in positive ways. The soldier's lot in war is self-sacrifice, in itself a virtue. And yet the essential business of war is killing and dying. It is a concerted attempt to do things that in times of peace we condemn utterly. War is a series of cruel and debasing acts undertaken on a massive scale, no matter how noble the ends these acts seek to achieve. Clearly, war is a failure to reach good ends by decent means. So both ideas about war are true. But where does that leave us?

One hopes, with a sense of conscience that does not overrule a sense of duty. One hopes, with a sense of duty that does not trump the decency of conscience. Put another way, we must be as good as we can possibly be while still bad enough to survive. At an even higher standard, we must be as good as we can possibly be while not abandoning our duty to others whose suffering we might alleviate, and whose continued existence we ought to aid when they are under threat. These are difficult tests, and to phrase them in this way is to provide not answers but perhaps questions rendered sharply enough to penetrate to the fundamental sense of justice and decency of those who hear them. That, in sum, is the project of Just War philosophy.

## THE MORAL EQUIVALENT OF WAR

A nation engaged in a war is a nation less concerned about trivia than about its values, its people, and its survival. William James wrote about this in his essay "The Moral Equivalent of War." Many modern readers approaching this essay for the first time assume that it will describe something as morally bad as war, but in fact it is James's attempt to imagine something as morally *good* as war. The essay settles on a proposal for required national service—a system like the Peace Corps or AmeriCorps—which would offer young people the good to be had from hard work and self-sacrifice in service to the nation without the accompanying obligations of war, to kill or die (for the most unlucky, to kill *and* die).

Beginning with this bit of wise humor, "The war against war is going to be no holiday excursion or camping party," "The Moral Equivalent of War" offers a tribal sensibility, with its celebration of the good that war does for men. James himself sits above these feelings, though. He describes them but does not endorse them. Writing in 1906, a generation after the Civil War, James felt sure of the attachment among Americans not only to the outcome of that war but to the very sufferings it brought to their parents and grandparents. "Ask all our millions, north and south," he wrote, "whether they would vote now (were such a thing possible) to have our war for the Union expunged from history, and the record of a peaceful transition to the present time substituted for that of its marches and battles, and probably hardly a handful of eccentrics would say yes. Those ancestors, those efforts, those memories and legends are the most ideal part of what we now own together, a sacred spiritual possession worth more than all the blood poured out." And James does not entirely disagree with this imagined consensus of American opinion. His project in the essay is to salvage the inherently positive aspects of men facing war, including the forging of "a sacred spiritual possession," from the larger wreck of war itself.

James's solution may seem simplistic. Could a peaceful few months or couple of years working on the railroad, building houses or dams, collecting plants in the desert or soil samples in the forest really give young men and women the kind of moral instruction that real battle provides? Likely not. Yet the intellectual value of James's proposal is significant. He is attempting to mediate between the older sense of war, anchored in war's virtue for the individual, and the modern sense, anchored in war's virtues for the group.

A generation earlier than James, John Stuart Mill expressed a more modern notion in 1862, also with the American Civil War in mind. "War is an ugly thing," Mill wrote in his essay "The Contest in America," "but not the ugliest of things. The decayed and degraded state of moral and patriotic feeling which thinks nothing worth fighting a war for, is worse." Mill rejects the tribal sense that war is noble, but he embraces the "moral and patriotic feeling"—the feeling that the individual feels in relation to his state—as a collective motive for war. (The title of an excellent book by the American journalist Christopher Hedges restates Mill's case in the language we use today to talk about ideas like moral and patriotic feeling: *War Is a Force That Gives Us Meaning*.) In Mill's case, the thing worth fighting for in America was the end of slavery. But the question that James asks is a shade more difficult than the question Mill answers. James asks the reader to suppose that the goal of the war might be met without the suffering of war. What if the slaves might have been freed and the Union preserved without a shot fired, a bone broken, or a single American field made gruesome with blood. Would we miss the war? Note that Mill sees the "moral and patriotic feeling" attached to war as a function of its goals and outcomes. Yet James sees those virtues in the very experience of war. Mill is saying that war is ugly but at times necessary. He seems to be in entire agreement with the thesis of this chapter, that war is always a failure but sometimes necessary. James is saying something more subtle: war is ugly, but it is beautiful too. Its virtues—not the virtues of a war's outcome but the virtues of the experience of war itself—are among the highest, even if its horrors are among the lowest.

If we choose to believe this, we can more easily accept that sometimes war is the best among awful alternatives. Indeed, a great deal of harm has been done in the twentieth century by leaders who seek to avoid war and preserve peace at all costs, no matter how ugly the state of things that war might overturn. More than a few moments in history reveal an abandonment of principle and of humane obligation to come to the aid of others who suffer, for the sake of forestalling war. These moments reveal little virtue among the peacemakers and more than a bit of harm borne by others for their efforts. Consider, for example, Europe in the 1930s and 1940s.

By 1938, Germany had fully emerged from its humiliation following the First World War. With Adolf Hitler as its head of state, a strong and aggressive military, and a broad civilian support for aggression across its borders, Germany threatened that September to invade Czechoslovakia. The Czech army was actually quite strong, and had it been backed by British and French forces it might have resisted Hitler and weakened the

Nazi regime in the process. So Hitler needed to isolate Czechoslovakia, to pull a strand apart from the nominal alliance of the Czechs, the British, and the French. With a victory against an isolated Czechoslovakia, he could then continue on to the British and the French, left without their former ally and thus no longer a match for the German military machine. Neville Chamberlain, then prime minister of England, has been remembered as a tragic figure because he chose the short-term ideal of peace over what virtually all later observers have seen as the ugly but necessary commitment to join with France and Czechoslovakia to fight Germany. That war would surely have brought with it some of the horror that began unfolding a year later, after Hitler invaded Poland (having taken all of Czechoslovakia earlier) and the rest of Europe understood that another world war had begun; but an earlier confrontation would likely have made of Hitler a militarist more on the scale of Slobodan Milosevic or Saddam Hussein—dangerous, murderous, but blocked from his fantasy of broad empire. But that was not the path chosen by Neville Chamberlain.

Duff Cooper, then England's first lord of the admiralty and author of the war memoir *Old Men Forget*, wrote about Chamberlain's report to the British cabinet on the notorious Munich agreement, signed by Chamberlain, French prime minister Edouard Daladier, Adolf Hitler, and Benito Mussolini, ceding the heart of Czechoslovakia to Germany.

> The Prime Minister looked none the worse for his experiences. He spoke for over an hour. He told us that Hitler had adopted a certain position from the start and had refused to budge an inch from it . . . [T]he prime minister concluded, to my astonishment, by saying that he considered that we

should accept those terms and that we should advise the Czechs to do so. It was then suggested that the cabinet should adjourn, in order to give members time to read the terms and sleep on them, and that we should meet again the following morning. I protested against this. I said that from what the Prime Minister had told us it appeared to me that the Germans were still convinced that under no circumstances would we fight, that there still existed one method, and one method only, of persuading them to the contrary, and that was by instantly declaring full mobilization.

But Chamberlain was determined to avoid war, at almost any cost. On September 30, 1938, he issued a joint statement with Hitler about the Munich agreement. It read, in part: "We regard the agreement signed last night and the Anglo-German Naval Agreement as symbolic of the desire of our two peoples never to go to war with one another again." Peace is so precious, and war so ugly. Yet in this case, the years that followed made it stunningly clear that, as John Stuart Mill had written eighty years earlier, though war is almost unthinkably awful, some things are worse than war. It is the burden of the head of state, the general, and the policy planner to choose between the things worse than war and war itself, and at times to say to citizens, "We must fight." That is not what Chamberlain said in a radio broadcast on September 27, three days before his joint announcement with Hitler. Instead he had this to say to his countrymen:

How horrible, fantastic, incredible it is that we should be digging trenches and trying on gas-masks here because of a quarrel in a far-away country between people of whom we know nothing! I would not hesitate to pay even a third visit to Germany, if I thought it would do any good.

Armed conflict between nations is a nightmare to me; but if I were convinced that any nation had made up its mind to dominate the world by fear of its force, I should feel that it must be resisted. Under such a domination, life for people who believe in liberty would not be worth living; but war is a fearful thing, and we must be very clear, before we embark on it, that it is really the great issues that are stake.

While waiting for further clarity, Chamberlain and Daladier chose to cede the Sudetenland of Czechoslovakia to Hitler, to choose an unjust peace over a war that might have done a great deal of good and forestalled the deaths of millions, the crushing of a dozen national governments, and the advent of industrial genocide.

A poignant echo of Chamberlain's humanitarian rhetoric can be found in an unexpected place—the 2001 Mitchell Report on the conflict between Israel and the Palestinians, prepared by a committee led by former U.S. senator George Mitchell and intended to set a context for renewed peace talks between Israel and the Palestinian Authority. In the report, Mitchell writes that "whatever the source, violence will not solve the problems of the region. It will only make them worse." Yet in this simple, almost naive statement, Mitchell captures the ugly quality of global peacemaking task forces, commissions, and bodies, the very kind that characterized the meeting among the European powers—England, France, Italy, and Germany—before Chamberlain's capitulation in the name of peace. From this global perspective on other people's struggles, the highest good is never justice but peace. Put another way, violence will not solve the problems of the Middle East for Mitchell and his fellow committeemen, because violence *is itself* the only real problem that will strike enough fear into the hearts of the world powers to motivate their peace missions.

Try, for example, to name a problem of concern to the global powers in the Occupied Territories, other than violence, that does not exist in extremis in at least three other Arab states. Interethnic hatred? Poor relations between Jews and Arabs? Lack of economic development? Police-statism? Clearly, what distinguishes the Territories is not the great problems there that have triggered violence, but the potentially destabilizing nature of the violence itself. The bombings, the killings of civilians, the threats of small incidents mushrooming into large scale, clash-of-civilizations war—that is the problem for Mitchell, the West, and those who focus their energies on smoothing the sands of Israel and Palestine. For Mitchell, the pronouncement that violence distracts from the ability of the rest of the world to aid in resolving the underlying problems is cynical to the extreme, because it is only the violence that turns the eyes and ears of the world's powers toward the Territories to begin with.

"There is only one way to peace, justice, and security in the Middle East, and that is through negotiation," the Mitchell Report goes on to assert, and a bald assertion it is: indeed, it is almost a plea, or a prayer, dressed in stern declarative prose. How does Mitchell know this to be true? In the notably few cases in which large-scale social conflicts have been settled through negotiation—the end of apartheid in South Africa is probably the most explicit example in modern history—close inspection reveals that a great deal of violence generally sets the stage for negotiation (tragically true in South Africa), and that the end result is more a stage reached in a long journey toward "peace, justice, and security" than the explicit delivery of these elusive ideals. The very next sentence in the report seems to close the case on Mitchell's will to believe in the unproven kindness of armed men: "Despite their long history and close proximity, some Israelis and Palestinians seem not to fully appreciate each other's concerns." This gentle language whispers that the crushingly obvious truth may perhaps exist: yes, Israelis and Palestinians have been killing each other for fifty years—or five hundred years or two thousand, depending on how you choose to define the key terms here (terms like "Israeli" and "Palestinian"). On each side it is not difficult to find people in positions of real power who openly confess that the men, women, and children of the other side may not deserve to live at all, and certainly not in the land over which they struggle. Do Mitchell and his committeemen not see this? Of course they do. But they seek peace, not truth, not justice, and like many statesmen—like Chamberlain—they choose to see less will to destruction than an ordinary man or woman would face with frightening clarity on the ground.

The point here is not to suggest any parallel between Nazi Germany and either of the forces in conflict in Israel and the Territories today, but instead to read Chamberlain and Mitchell together, and to recognize the common expression they share of abhorring war and wanting peace to such a degree that they will pretend it may exist even where it cannot. They untether violence from its causes, its outcomes, and its claim to justice. The combatants readily recognize this, while the great-power custodians of the status quo seek to preserve peace at any cost, no matter how ugly the lives of men and women left behind, lives not at war, not at struggle, but held still under the arms of those who claim to govern.

Thus the idea that war, though always wrong, is sometimes necessary. Nevertheless, war is always a strategic failure for all but the most brutal regimes. The nation contemplating a war of defense has failed to secure its borders by other means—by means, that is, that will not require the slaughter of young men in uniform, and men, women, and children who by doing no more than living their lives inevitably die as the victims, often unintended, of war. The nation contemplating a war to further its aims abroad has failed to further those aims by other means. But has the nation that finds itself contemplating war for the sake of empire or plunder actually failed? It chooses war for its own aims, to reach its goals faster and more fully than those aims might be satisfied by other means. The historian or the scholar of civilizations might say no, this nation has not failed in its own aims. Yet this question requires a moral judgment, and it is not difficult to make that judgment. That nation has failed too; it has failed to be decent and to protect and preserve the lives of its citizens (to say nothing of the citizens of other nations it sets out to kill). And so one can say with ease that all war is failure. At times it is a failure of a nation's own aims. Always it is a failure to live up to the vision of the state that emerged in the 1700s—the state with a duty to its own citizens and to the world.

But how, if always a failure, can war sometimes be necessary? The classic moral diagram of Just War is built of three parties: one's own state, an aggressor state, and an innocent third party, perhaps a state, perhaps a group of stateless people, perhaps citizens of the aggressor state. The duty to come to the aid of the innocent party is itself a justification for war, just as literal and direct self-defense is a justification. The failure to prevent these situations from unfolding may be reason for national self-condemnation, but that failure is not reason for paralysis. The choice here is not between right and wrong but between two wrongs—the wrong of a war and all the killing it implies, and the wrong to come if war is not undertaken: innocent people will suffer, and the aggressor nation will not be restrained and weakened. The reason to fight Hitler's Germany when it moved on Czechoslovakia in 1938, or when it took Poland in 1939, for example, was not only to protect the innocents of that nation who eventually perished at German hands but also to constrain the German war machine, to weaken it, and to establish the fact that, no, the world would not stand still as one nation struck at others for the sake of empire.

Some nations did declare war on Germany in 1939, though the United States was not among them. Had it been, perhaps the history of the Second World War would finally have been less bloody. Yet our nation, like most nations, has seldom made war only for the motives that Just War theories suggest. In fact, the wars of this century that we celebrate most—the Second World War and the Gulf War—combined motives of decency (stopping Nazis, saving the innocent, toppling dictators, standing up against empire building) with the most practical issues of self-interest (the need for a stable Europe in the first case, and the need for oil in the second). Were these wars, too, failures? Yes, they were. Our nation failed to take less dramatic action earlier that would certainly have limited these wars, and might well have prevented them. Had the United States aided Republican Spain, or France, or England earlier—the list is endless— Germany might well have been contained or even defeated far earlier in the conflict, and with many millions fewer dead in Europe and Africa. Had the United States not aided Saddam Hussein as a convenient ally against a mutual enemy, or recognized

the validity of the Kurdish people's movement in Iraq; or consistently opposed anti-democratic regimes throughout the Middle East—again, the list does not end—we might well have
forestalled the invasion of Kuwait and the rush to arms to expel
Iraq's imperialistic land grab. In the end, both wars served good
ends (among other ends perhaps less good), but both wars also
represented years of closed eyes, weak will, and failed commit-
ments to democratic ideals on the part of our nation and others.
And so it always is with war, except for those nations that embrace it in principle. For all others, war is failure. And even for
the warmongers, war is a failure too—a failure of legitimacy in
an age in which the divine right of kings has fallen away and
every flicker of modern culture that penetrates even the most
cloistered nations speaks loudly of the rights, the potency, and
the power of the individual.

# 2

# THE FUNDAMENTAL IDEAS
# OF JUST WAR

CARL VON CLAUSEWITZ is probably the best-known writer on war. His world was the world of men under arms. Born in 1780, Clausewitz was a boy soldier, lucky to survive his first battles as a near-useless uniformed child who might at least slow an enemy's advance. Grown to a station of middling influence by dint of hundreds of battles and decades of military training and leadership, Clausewitz produced a set of ideas about war among the best informed of any writer's. He offers immense insights into the causes, functions, and execution of war but little application of those insights to the questions of why to fight and why not to. But Clausewitz is clearly an essential link in the chain of serious thought about war, in part because of the life he lived and in part because of his subtle recording of the most profound changes in the relation of war to the state. Those changes had little to do with how men fight and much to do with the changing nature of the state.

The late eighteenth century was such a dramatic time for the rise and fall of nations, political systems, and the very ideas of what states could and should be that many of the philosophers of the period whose work survives take up the question of the state, and directly or indirectly they take up the question of war as well. Clausewitz and Georg Wihelm Friedrich Hegel—building in part on Immanuel Kant—describe the rise of the modern state in their philosophical writings. Both speak of the state as an entity with appetite and will, and lay the foundation for the modern idea that war is the drama of states in conflict.

Clausewitz began his military career in 1793 at the age of twelve, when he became a lance corporal in the Prussian army. He saw his first battles fighting the French. In 1801 he entered the Prussian War College, and when he graduated in 1803 he went to work as military adviser to a Prussian prince. In 1806, Prussia was defeated by France, and Clausewitz found himself in a French jail. Eventually freed, he made his way back to Prussia in 1808. By 1812 he had signed on to the Russian army, glad to be able to fight Napoleon's French forces again as the alliance between France and Russia dissolved. Clausewitz helped Prussia and Russia join in a military alliance, and in 1815 he returned to service as an officer in the Prussian army. All along, Clausewitz was assembling a wide-ranging set of notes that, by the late 1820s, amounted to a highly practical philosophy of war.

Hegel, ten years older than Clausewitz, certainly had a strong influence on the younger man's thinking and writing, though Clausewitz might have had something to say about Hegel's general avoidance of arms (in Napoleon's victory over Prussian troops in the town of Jena in 1806, Hegel was famously lodged in a cellar, waiting for the battle to pass). Hegel's fundamental contribution to the understanding of history was what he called dialectical progression. History, Hegel wrote, is the motion of forces and ideas encountering movements that oppose them. Eventually compromise positions are created, and they themselves become new forces that in turn encounter their own opposition. Thus his famous formula for the progress of history: thesis meets antithesis, and the two form a synthesis. The synthesis becomes a thesis itself, meets its own antithesis, and so on. Hegel applied this model specifically to European states and mapped out his three-step, forward-moving dance of history explicitly: states embody social, economic, and cultural ideas which give rise to their own opposition. The opposing forces—be they groups of men with arms, or ideas intent on undermining social norms—rub against orthodoxies with varying degrees of bluster and bloodshed, and from these encounters new orthodoxies—even new states—emerge. Hegel's innovation in seeing states as ever-changing creatures was more dramatic in its time that it may seem to a twenty-first-century reader, and it took a degree of courage. After all, Hegel was essentially declaring that all current states would be fleeting entities, and that no current ruler would rule forever or leave an unchanging legacy. In an era of absolute monarchy, this was a notably dangerous idea. Was Hegel, after all, declaring that the Prussian state was less than perfect, destined to be reshaped by some antithesis, some more socially advanced revolutionary movement? An honest reader would have to say yes, that's the general idea of Hegel's philosophy of history. But the great man himself took the time to append a chapter to his most important book to say that of course these profound ideas applied only to the past, and that the Prussian state was history's final evolutionary stopping point. Cynical but practical, Hegel was thus seen as a friend of the Prussian royals. That his writings proposed the first systematic—rather than merely philosophical—rejection of divine monarchy in Europe escaped their notice, preoccupied as they were with fighting the French.

Clausewitz and Hegel, however they felt about the idea of divine monarchy, were most excited by the idea that states by their nature were constantly changing. War for both was a natural thing, not a product of evil threatening good but of states exercising their appetites and quite simply doing what states do. The idea of natural law was not particularly interesting to either. To the extent that justice operates at all in either's view of the state, it operates as a matter of understanding—of seeing the motion of states correctly—rather than of alignment with a fixed idea of the absolute good.

Writing a generation before Hegel and Clausewitz, Kant had created a body of work that was enormously important in laying the groundwork for the younger men's writings. Yet Kant's central concern remains the individual. Kant is an idealist because he is concerned entirely with the moral life of the individual, and he considers the state only in the context of that moral life. This makes Kant a remarkable transitional figure between the tribal view of war and the modern. He sees that states have shape and structure, and that wars are affairs that have at least as much to do with states as with individuals. But the meaning of these wars he considers only from the perspective of individual experience. The story of the individual is still the only story he is particularly interested in.

Although Hegel and Clausewitz build upon Kant, they take very different starting points. Clausewitz writes about war because he is a warrior. His writings consider war from the broadest perspectives and therefore address just about every aspect of human behavior; but his motivating question is simple: How can an army fight with the greatest prospect of victory? Hegel, writing at roughly the same time as Clausewitz and within the same social and cultural world, begins at the other extreme. His motivating question is vast: How does history work?

Yet both these questions rest on an even more fundamental idea, the idea of the state. Ideas about the purpose and nature of the state were very much in the air in the late eighteenth and early nineteenth centuries, many of them put there by Jean-Jacques Rousseau. A Swiss-born French philosopher twelve years older than Kant, Rousseau's work asked at every turn, What is the state? Rousseau had an ideal view of the "state of nature" that he thought existed before men and women came together in groups, tribes, and eventually states, but he nevertheless saw a powerful and positive moral benefit from the state. The fair and just state, Rousseau wrote in *The Social Contract*, "produces a remarkable change in man, by substituting justice for instinct in his conduct, and giving his actions the morality they had formerly lacked." He saw war as a failure—"Anyone can see that aggressive rulers wage war at least as much on their subjects as on their enemies, and that the conquering nation is left no better off than the conquered"—though he did not rule out its necessity. Rousseau was enough of a realist to know that, at times, failure to fight might be yet worse. Yet he was essentially a critic, seeking to understand and speak out against the potential excesses of government. His writings on war argued that reflection and restraint were sorely lacking in most nations' conduct in choosing, planning, and fighting their wars, and explicitly grounded the legitimacy of any government and any war in the universal and absolute rights of man.

The whole of Rousseau's written work shows a restless mind, a great faith in the better angels of man's nature, and a sense of proportion in the exercise of power. Most important, in typically exuberant prose he called for balance, measure, and restraint in the exercise of state power.

All these thinkers have one important quality in common: for each, the moral scale of war is large. They raise moral and material questions that involve large groups of men and women, large pieces of geography, and broad cultural and social implications. And yet with only one exception there is little room for the individual as a moral actor in this newly emerging view. The tribal view of war made the individual soldier or warrior the central actor—perhaps unreflective but still central—while this emerging modern notion of war left the individual almost entirely out in practical terms. Deeply engaged as these thinkers were with questions of the state—and as distinctly as their ideas of statecraft championed the rights of individuals—their concerns were structural and organizational. They were high-level thinkers, wrestling with new questions about the large-scale elements of human society. With one exception, the private, interior life of the individual man or woman was not their subject.

Kant is that exception. While Hegel and others take from Kant his willingness to pass moral judgment on states, and to see states as redeemable even in their worst failings, they do not take up Kant's intense interest in the moral character and moral progress of the individual. In fact, Kant's seldom-studied writings about war argue that men who lead nations in times of war must retain sufficient moral integrity to govern once the fighting ends. He is concerned about how the souls of those men affect the policies of the state. This concern also reveals (though indirectly) the modern presumption that war is a temporary abrogation of decency for the sake of more decent ends. While war rages, Kant wants the warriors to think about the peace that will follow. It is a sterling example of Kant's habit of looking, always, at the individual as a moral force.

Immanuel Kant was born, lived, and seems never to have left the provincial capital city of Königsberg in East Prussia (in its last years under this name, the city was the home of the twentieth-century philosopher Hannah Arendt; with the advent of Soviet East Germany, it became the rather grim city of Kaliningrad). He was born to working parents who were quite religious. Ordinarily a boy with this background would not have been able to live much of an intellectual life in eighteenth-century Prussia, but Kant was befriended by a preacher who admired his mother, and he was granted special admission to a religious high school in Königsberg, where his extraordinary intellect was noted and his admission to the University of Königsberg arranged. Even with his university degree, though, money remained a practical concern for Kant. He held a prestigious post as a popular lecturer in religion and philosophy for fifteen years, but the position was unpaid. He earned his living tutoring the children of the wealthy, a compromise adequate for a man who lived his entire adult life as a bachelor. That compromise lasted until 1770 when Kant was awarded the chair of logic and metaphysics at the university, and finally found himself among the few leading professors there who were paid for their labors.

## GROTIUS AND SECULAR MORALITY

Kant's thinking about war was greatly influenced by the seventeenth-century Dutch statesman Hugo Grotius.

Grotius did his most important work in the years following the Thirty Years War and the reconfiguration of the borders of

Europe, including the grant of independence to his own nation. In an era of change not unlike that following the First World War in the twentieth century, Grotius articulated fundamental principles of government that sat above the monarch but below the heavens. He devised a theory of international law based on the good that states do to those whom they govern, laying the foundation for the European Enlightenment that would be built upon by Hegel, Rousseau, and the political philosophy of John Locke. Most important, Grotius wrote that the purpose of Just War thinking was not to achieve the goals of the state better or more efficiently, or to aid man in his struggle to comprehend and obey the will of God, but rather to offer "succor and protection for the sick and wounded in war, combatants and civilians alike."

Thus Grotius was especially interested in the ideas of *how* an army fights—adding to the broader criteria that Aquinas codified for *when* to fight. In particular, Grotius helped to codify the ideas of distinguishing between soldiers and civilians in battle, and the proportionality of acts of war, that is, that the harm done in battle be in proportion to the good to come from victory. These innovations in thinking gave a voice to the secular experience of moral thought, and liberated the benevolent intentions of statesmen and citizens who wished to make their states better, and to make their policies more decent, but did not particularly wish to follow the orthodoxies of any church in their public exercise of power. Grotius was a particularly strong influence on Locke, who articulated directly what Grotius had said only indirectly: that the civilian population of an enemy state bears no responsibility for the hostile acts of its leadership, and indeed holds inalienable rights and freedoms that cannot be fairly abridged even if defeated, invaded, or otherwise vanquished. The lineage from Grotius to Locke to Jefferson is especially important for students of American history and for those who wish to make sense of the various American approaches to justifying war. But the quiet Prussian, Immanuel Kant, is the philosophical master of all the figures who come after Grotius.

Kant's writings, like those of Grotius, share an inclination to ask the same fundamental moral questions that religions take up but to answer them apart from any church orthodoxies. In Kant's case, his path is the experience of the individual as an individual, while the path of Grotius is the path of the state in relation to its moral obligation to the individual. Yet the humane spirit and the respect for the integrity of the individual is the same. A door opens in Grotius's work, and Kant walks through it, clarifies the idea of the moral integrity of the individual, and centers his work on it.

Still, Kant is more than an idealist. In his writings on war, in particular, there is a practical streak that brings to mind the intellectual toughness of Aquinas. Kant's overall moral philosophy rests on his notion of the "categorical imperative," the moral principle that the individual adopts and adheres to as a matter of free will and reflective thought, and sees as a good for every man and woman to follow. Kant's categorical imperative is categorical not only because the individual is to adhere to it under all conditions, but because the individual wants everyone else, in all other circumstances, to adhere to it too. There is an elegant balance of individualism and commitment to the common good in this notion: the individual freely chooses what to believe, but he chooses only among options that are good for all—that is, options that are mutually beneficial.

When he turns his attention directly to the question of war,

Kant seems undecided about when a state is right to fight. He sees a nation as justified in entering a war if it has been wronged, but he does not account for problems of poor judgment, realpolitik, and simple misperception as nations inspect themselves with an eye toward declaring their own status as victims. On the questions of how a nation is to fight, Kant sees the connection between a war and the peace to follow it: he demands high restraint so that the inevitable victor may have the moral authority to preside over a just peace. "Defensive measures and means of all kinds are allowable to a state that is forced to war," he writes, "except such as by their use would make the subjects using them unfit to be citizens; for the state would thus make itself unfit to be regarded as a person capable of participating in equal rights in the international relations according to the right of nations." Like Clausewitz, Kant uses the metaphor of a man for the state. And he assigns the motives of a man to the state. Unlike Clausewitz, he does not assign honor or appetite or will to the state—these do not interest Kant terribly much. Instead he imputes reason and moral fitness, the two notions that Kant loves most to consider. More to the point, he concentrates on that space in which reason and moral fitness converge. The state at war acts most reasonably and most morally when exercising restraint and respect for its enemies, much as the categorical imperative itself requires the individual who freely chooses a moral principle to consider the actions of all others in making that choice. In fact, Kant puts quite plainly a definition of Just War that is nothing more than a scaling-to-state-size of the categorical imperative: "But what then," he asks, "is an unjust enemy according to the conceptions of the right of nations, when, as holds generally of the state of nature, every state is judge of its own cause? It is one whose publicly expressed will, whether in word or deed, betrays a maxim which, if it were taken as a universal rule, would make a state of peace among the nations impossible, and would necessarily perpetuate the state of nature."

A nation is wrong, he is saying, if it acts on principles—maxims—that serve self-interest but not common interest. The nation is wrong if it is led into war by principles that, if other nations followed them, would lead away from peace and order, and toward domination of the many by the few.

Kant's moral philosophy has a great deal less to do with the individual making peace than with the fact of living among others. Something is good for the individual only if it is good for all individuals. And so it is perhaps inevitable that Kant's thinking about war leads him to the idea of world government, or what he called "a universal union of states." "It may be said," Kant concludes at the end of his *Metaphysical Elements of Justice*, "that the universal and lasting establishment of peace constitutes not merely a part, but the whole final purpose and end of the science of right as viewed within the limits of reason." And that "science of right" is what Kant considers to be his entire project as a thinker and writer. All his work, he is saying, all his struggle to understand the world, is in fact the struggle toward peace. Yet Kant's final conclusions ring somewhat hollow. "A just enemy," he writes, "would be one to whom I would do no wrong in offering resistance; but such a one would really not be my enemy." Indeed. War is not fought among states or peoples who share a common moral outlook. It is fought among nations that feel their enemies are not worthy—not worthy to live in some cases, or perhaps not worthy to hold the ground they hold. Just as the truism of Political Science 101 that democratic states never have wars with one another falls apart when we begin to consider just which state is *really* democratic, any decent Just War theory ought to keep just nations, governed by legitimate authorities and motivated by right motives, from ever facing each other in battle—if only we could be sure what states are the truly good ones. The Jihadi, the Christian Soldier, the Defender of the Faith fill the world with war precisely to settle those questions with which Just War doctrine begins: What government is legitimate? And what cause is right?

Even Kant, with his purity of heart and depth of intellect, gives us only questions and no real answers beyond the dream of world government, which is itself merely a restatement of the problem: if only the world will come together peaceably under one flag, there will be no war. Yes, but the question of how to get all nations to that point in good faith *is the very same question* of how to get them to stop making war with one another in the first place.

Kant's writing, always concerned with the spiritual experience of ordinary men, was largely impenetrable to all but the most sophisticated and patient readers. He was a man concerned with a fairly narrow—but deep—range of ideas, with no interest in a wide audience, and with little apparent concern for the world beyond his quiet town in East Prussia. Nevertheless it is Kant, a generation older than Hegel and Clausewitz, who points to the most obvious flaw in the modern, state-centered notion of war: it has too little to say about the individual. In the twenty-first century we have so fully digested the essential teachings of Hegel and Clausewitz about war, the state, and the large movements of history that we too need to awaken to the central role of the individual that Kant asserts. Considered in the context of Just War thinking, Kant is a voice of balance and of sensitivity to the small scale of individual experience, even as we engage in the large-scale thinking of Just War tradition. Yes, there has been a shift in the balance of moral thinking about war as human society has moved from the ancient to the modern, but we risk a loss of the humane if we do not seek some integration of both.

## THE MORAL STATE AND
## THE IDEA OF NATURAL LAW

Particularly in light of the increasing importance of the state in the way we think about war, we must ask, How does a state act morally? The most enduring model of moral action by states falls neatly under the heading of natural law philosophy. Natural law philosophy describes a relationship among the state, the individual, and God (by some name or another) in which the state is essentially the agent of God in bringing a set of right standards to the life of the individual. The innovation of the earliest forms of natural law philosophy was to make the ultimate standard of state action something other than power. Rather than might making right, natural law proposes that right preexists, and that the good state serves that right.

The Roman orator Cicero articulated the idea of natural law well, though by the time this idea began to dominate the modern world through the writings of Rousseau, Locke, and Thomas Jefferson, it meant something very different. It was no longer the natural law of a God (or gods) working through the state. Cicero wrote that "True law is right reason in agreement with nature. It is of universal application, unchanging and everlasting." In contrast, Jefferson said in 1801, in his first inaugural address, that "a wise and frugal government" is one that "shall restrain men from injuring one another, . . . shall leave them otherwise free to regulate their own pursuits of industry and improvement, and shall not take from the mouth of labor the bread it has earned." The difference in tone reveals a great deal. Cicero sees the state's role as pervasive and the state itself as a font of goodness. Jefferson sees the state's role as necessary but in need of restraint, and the good state as one that checks and limits its own influence in the life of the individual. In the centuries separating these men, natural law changed from a force restraining the individual to a force restraining the state. In large part this was because the state itself had moved beyond its premodern function—best summed up somewhat after the fact by Thomas Hobbes—of protecting man from the wildness of the world and from his own frightening nature, to the more modern function summed up by Jefferson, of governing best by governing least. Jefferson still worried about man's nature (thus his idea that the state must "restrain men from injuring one another"), but he saw man less as a beast to be restrained than as a creature of great potential cultivation, to be given the proper environment and then set free. It was government itself that he saw as the source of wild impulses. In a 1787 letter to Edward Carrington he wrote, "If once [the people] . . . become inattentive to public affairs, you and I, and Congress and Assemblies, Judges and Governors, shall all become wolves."

Philosophies of natural law set on restraining the state rather than restraining the individual begin with the idea that the state is a powerful and dynamic thing—a modern notion that finds clear expression in Jefferson's work and may well be one of his most important ideas. Others had written about the encroaching habits of kings, rulers, and agents of the state, but Jefferson centered his life's work on the need to restrain the habits of the state itself, not only the habits of the men at the helm of the state. Thus while others might write that the problem with a particular king or provincial ruler was his heavy-handedness, it was Jefferson, building on Rousseau and Locke, who said plainly that it was in the nature of states to want to do too much with, for, and to the people, and thus they must be continually held back from their own inclination.

This idea of the state having its own appetites becomes even more important a generation later, in the work of Clausewitz and Hegel. Unlike Cicero—or Plato—Clausewitz and Hegel see the state in terms of its motion, a motion created by unsatisfied appetites. They see war within the context of this motion, as an expression of the state's appetite. War, for Hegel and Clausewitz, was a tool for expanding and rejuvenating the state, an inevitable function of history's motion, in which the state played the primary role. For Cicero, war was tied to a sense of the state's goodness. Justice was the cause and the goal of the good state, and its wars reflected its progress toward that fixed end. But Cicero had a narrow sense of justice. His notion of justice was God's justice, a matter of pious self-evidency. The job of the state for Cicero was to find its point of alignment with natural law and then stay there, and in his time and place that kind of a good government was sorely needed (though whether it was possible—Jefferson would argue that it was never possible—was another question). Cicero's moral vision shows the weakness—some might say the hypocrisy—of those too well pleased with their own goodness.

In Cicero's view, the good may preserve their goodness even by lying: the goodness of the individual actor, even as he lies, can trump the fact of the lie. "Imagine, for example," Cicero writes, "that you have been captured by pirates, and you agree with them to pay a ransom for your life. Yet even if your agreement had been an oath, your failure to deliver the ransom would not count as fraudulent. For a pirate does not come into the category of regular enemies since he is the enemy of all the world—as far as he is concerned, good faith and oaths do not come into the picture at all." Identity is more important than action here—the good may lie because they are good. Sin against the bad does not count, because they are bad. For Cicero there is no grey area. His philosophy of the state presumes that the state has full knowledge of the souls of men. Cicero's state has all it needs: knowledge of the souls of men and knowledge of right standards in God's (of the gods') eyes. Cicero follows the lead of Plato's *Republic* in this model of the all-knowing state which, because of its knowledge of the hearts of men, is excused for small acts of dishonesty and indecency. In Plato's *Republic*, the state decides who shall enjoy political leadership and who shall become craftsmen, soldiers, and workmen, and it propagates myths about the physical stuff contained in the bodies of each caste in order to explain each man's fixed status. In other words, the state lies to its citizens to ensure their easy compliance with pervasive sacrifice and restrictions meant to serve the common good.

Plato's republic was a fiction, an imagined place. Some even argue that it was a world made so extreme as to be an argument against itself (this is the ironic reading of Plato, that he-can't-be-serious reading). But Cicero was talking about a real place, the state in which he himself was a functionary, the state as he found it or as it could be in the short term. Plato dreamed and reasoned; Cicero governed. But Cicero's state is a static state. The state as he presents it lacks dynamism precisely because of Cicero's moral presumption of the ability to judge the souls of the citizenry, both personally and on behalf of the state. Cicero does not imagine a need to restrain the state, or to fear the state, on behalf of the individual. Thus it is no great surprise that Cicero's most distinct contribution to Just War philosophy is the idea that a just war must be waged by a state, rather than a tribe or clan, and further, that war can only be just "once an official demand for satisfaction has been submitted or warning has been given and a formal declaration made." State-centric, bound up in process and protocol, Cicero's clear statement of this principle represents a distinct point of transition from the tribal idea of war to the modern.

Cicero's ideas are part of a Greco-Roman tradition first presented by the Greek historian Thucydides in *The Peloponnesian War*, in the chapter known as the Melian Dialogue. In that dialogue, representatives of a formidable force of ships, men, horses, and arms from Athens approach the leaders of the island of Melos, a loose ally of the Spartans, after the Athenians have set up camp on the island with the clear intent to conquer. The Athenians expect to address a crowd of civilians, to argue that resistance would be suicide, and to secure a quick surrender. But the Melian leaders have in mind a more thoughtful exchange with the Athenians. They seem to think they can forestall the Athenian invasion through the strength of their moral position and the clarity of their arguments. The Athenians are skeptical. "You know as well as we do," they say, "that right, as the world goes, is only in question between equals in power, while the strong do what they can and the weak suffer what they must." The Melians reply that their right to make a moral case for peace—not the peace of conquest but the peace of independence—is "our common protection," a principle of natural law that applies to strong states as well as weak. The Athenians hear them out and then leave, asking the Melians to consider the opportunity to surrender. The Melians reply that surrender is impossible, that "we will not in a moment deprive of freedom a city that has been inhabited these seven hundred years; but we put our trust in the fortune by which gods have preserved it until now. . . . We invite you to allow us to be friends with you . . . and to retire from our country after making such a treaty as shall seem fit to us both." At first the Athenians are distracted by battles on other islands. But a few months later they set about to defeat the Melians, who finally surrender after a prolonged siege. The Athenians, Thucydides tells his readers, "put to death all the grown men whom they took, and sold the women and children for slaves, and subsequently sent out five hundred colonists and inhabited the place themselves."

The cruel outcome of this episode is far less a surprise than the extended drama of the dialogue itself, filled as it is with serious ideas. Why would the Athenians delay to hear their target's philosophy of government? An immediate surrender would have saved them time and trouble, though not particularly much, given their overwhelming power. The dialogue seems to be something of a tribute to the Melians' notion that a people's arguments ought to be heard—that the exchange of ideas is a precious "common protection," and that the conduct of nations is as important as the lives or deaths of individuals. Two earlier episodes of Greek history laid something of a foundation for this impulse of Greek statecraft. The first was recorded by the writer Strabo close to the year 1 A.D. but took place about seven hundred years earlier, when warring Greek armies agreed to rules of war that limited the range of weapons they would use. The second took place roughly a hundred years later, when the Greeks, victorious in the First Sacred War, looked back over the brutality that had brought them victory and recorded a promise not to use access to food and water as a tool of war against other Greeks. By Homer's time, these self-imposed restrictions, and others like them, were known as the "common customs of battle." They were clearly a part of what makes the ancient Greek and Roman worlds so appealing for the modern West—the notion that ancient though those empires were, the seeds of our modern civic life were indeed sown there.

Cicero surely would have read Thucydides, Homer, and many other writers who recorded these traditions. His requirement for a formal declaration of war, and an opportunity for the target state to respond, seems to take the lesson of the Melian Dialogue and extend it from history, as Thucydides preserves it, to philosophy and policy, as Cicero wished to contemplate and practice it.

A contemporary of Julius Caesar, Cicero lived through the first great period of empire in world history, yet the imperial city of Rome saw little stability during Cicero's adult life in the first century B.C. Petty rebellions were frequent in and around Rome; pirates raided the Italian coast and at times the port of Rome itself; and wars of empire and resistance were common. The Roman state relentlessly expanded its reach, but its wars were disjointed, its ruling class often divided against itself, and its culture often weak within the city and weaker still as it radiated outward through the empire. Travel was largely by foot, and communications were no faster. Rome was an empire, but it was never of one piece, never a cohesive whole. The messiness of the physical world, of an empire filled with half a hundred languages and cultures, lurks behind Cicero's prose. His state is so knowing and certain that a soldier taken hostage by pirates is not bound by his word. Is this a portrait of a state so sure of its rightness that, like the ideal state in Plato's *Republic*, lies in service to the common good are no cause for alarm because everyone understands that the state itself and the men who run it are perfectly good? Or is this a portrait of a state beset by pirates and kidnappers struggling to keep itself whole? Perhaps it is both. Perhaps the emphasis on statecraft and due diplomatic process in the making of war strengthens the state, giving it a central role in war as a partial answer to skeptics who question why the state exists at all, in addition to serving other moral aims. For Cicero and his conception of natural law, strengthening the state serves the greater moral good because the state is itself a vessel of goodness. To believe this is to place the good of the state above the good of the individual, a common enough act but a dangerous one.

For Cicero, personal and public virtue are tightly bound together. Both are matters of reflection, restraint, and duty—virtues that served well amidst the uncertainties of Cicero's Rome. Although Cicero's ideal state might gain or lose territory, the motive of discovery plays only a small part in his worldview. In Cicero's lifetime Rome was largely a preservationist state rather than an outward-looking one. It sought to capture the world and bring the spoils to Rome rather than go into the world and be changed by it. And so the wars of Rome in Cicero's time reflected the static qualities of personal virtue in Cicero's writings: the empire might become greater or weaker, the individual might be more virtuous or less, but the nature of the state and the nature of man were not open to questions. Virtue was not fluid. Man and the state struggled to become virtuous, but they did not struggle to improve—to risk—their standards of virtue. There was risk enough in the air as it was. In the world Cicero presents, the citizen does not need to be protected from the state because the citizen has little important work to do, little creative social function, that the state might interfere with. The citizen's own notion of virtue is irrelevant to public life, because virtue is not being shaped, renewed, or renovated by the individual. Virtue is duty. The state dominates the individual, the individual serves the state, and war is a matter of gaining territory, suppressing rebellion, and preserving the privileges of Rome. The strong will dominate the weak, but they will do so with a degree of decorum, exercising diplomacy and turning a face to the world that reveals the collective and coordinated powers of the state. Wars were required to begin well in addition to ending well, so that victory belonged not to the strong arm of the soldier but to Rome.

## THE CHRISTIAN CITY OF ROME

By the time Augustine conceived his City of God, beginning in 413 A.D., Rome was a different place than it had been in Cicero's day. Perhaps most important, it was a Christian city. In the year 306, Constantine became emperor of Rome. Thought by many to have been a believer most of his life, Constantine's commitment to Christianity was unclear until the year 312, when the Roman historian Lactantius reports that Constantine had a dream before a battle. In the dream, Roman soldiers marked their shields with crosses. A later historian, Eusebius, told the story that Constantine then saw a cross in the sky and heard the words, "By this you shall conquer." Rome prevailed in the battles of 312, and in 313, Constantine declared the toleration of Christianity throughout the empire. An era of church building began, with particular effect in Jerusalem and surrounding towns, including Bethlehem. By 315 the Roman world had become the first Christian empire. Constantine, now a Christian, continued to fight and conquer under the cross he believed had led him to victory in battle.

About forty years later, Augustine of Hippo was born. If his *Confessions* are to be believed, for many of his early years Augustine lived a life of pleasure and indulgence. He became a Christian in the year 386 and laid the groundwork for a new kind of Christianity, not a Christianity of the manger or a Christianity of the margins but a Christianity of the world, even a Christianity of the state. Written from 413 to 426, Augustine's *City of God* wrestles with the role of civil governance in relation to the church and, more specifically, the role of the church in relation to Rome. In 410, Goths had sacked Rome, and a number of influential politicians laid blame for Rome's devastating losses on the empire's turn to the Christian faith and away from the traditional pagan gods. Augustine set out to refute them.

In *City of God*, Augustine talks a good deal about the role of individual will. The very idea of individualism takes a historic step into the light through Augustine's work. He tries to strike a balance, using the faith-filled contradiction of free will in a universe ordained by God, between the absolutes of faith and the realities of life as lived in the world. A rebel faith has little need for these compromises, because it is far from power. But a state religion must make its compromises, and from that need Augustine begins the Christian Just War tradition.

Perhaps most important in Augustine's view of war was that the good Christian could fight only on one side. That is to say, his sense of war went beyond and above duty, and presupposed that one side in a Just War would be wrong and the other right—or at least right enough. Loyalty to family, state—and one supposes to church—would never be enough to make a soldier's service just; the larger cause must be just. This idea represents an enormous leap beyond the tribal notions of war as one man's story regardless of the larger conflict, and war as an inevitable act in the larger drama of a people's survival. Although a Roman inclined to render unto Caesar what was Caesar's, Augustine saw the moral failure of empire. "[T]he very extent of the empire itself," he wrote, "has produced wars of a more obnoxious description—social and civil wars—and with those the whole race has been agitated, either by actual conflict or fear of a renewed outbreak." It was not enough to trust wise men to wage wise wars, he continued. The morality of war was not a matter of wisdom but of moral righteousness. It was not a matter of empire but a matter of decency. But in the question of what qualifies as decency lay Augustine's own great compromise, the idea that war itself could be peaceful, that the soldier at arms could be Christ-like. Augustine's ideas challenged Rome, but they also blessed Rome more or less as it was, the seat of an empire very much in flux and always, somewhere, at war.

Still, Augustine's Rome resembles Cicero's in several key aspects. Most important, Augustine's Christian ethics share with Cicero's classical Roman notion of the gods the older natural law equation: the role of the state is to help the individual adhere to the right, which is to say, to the will of God. Because in this view the good is static, and the state's highest function is to bring the practical aspects of the good into the lives of ordinary people, the ideal state is static too. The state seeks, in essence, to serve God. To the extent that progress and discovery are part of the common good that the state provides and protects, they are an inward-looking process. The object of discovery is not the new but the old—not the world but the virtues of godliness.

The good lies upward in heaven or inward in the soul, not outward in the world. The state's greatest function is to aid God's purpose of bringing people to right living and the love of virtue. That is the core of what states do in Cicero's and Augustine's worlds.

The twenty-first-century reader is likely to find the simplicity of this vision of the state's obligation to the public good charming, and also disturbing. Charming because the classical conception of the state is comforting—if only it were so, our lives would be so much easier. Disturbing because too often states cling to the total authority that generally comes with this notion of natural law, and they repress the habit of the governed to point to the state's failings and incompleteness. In other words, trouble arises when citizens seek to put the state into motion by effecting change, or to reveal the fact that the state already *is* in motion, is in fact changing. The state is offended by any such idea, preferring to see itself as the ultimate state rather than merely the best we can manage at a given moment.

Thus the revolutionary modernity of Hegel and Clausewitz: they saw a world of states in motion, they understood that change was not only inevitable but in some ways its own cause. States would not stand still, would not reach natural end points, but would by their very natures change and change again. Wars would come not because of principles, not because of God's will or the greater glory of essential ideas, but because war is a fundamental expression of the unavoidable will of the state. All of which leaves us back at the question with which we began: How do states act morally?

A compelling set of answers revolves, again, around the question of will. Perhaps the most powerful voice in the history of philosophy to speak on the question of will was the thirteenth-century churchman Thomas Aquinas—though he spoke against it. Aquinas places Will—he capitalizes it, making it almost a small god, or anti-god, of its own right—at the root of the kind of individualism, full of appetite, that he fights at every turn. If will is a motivating force, even a necessary one, Aquinas must fill the hole he creates by vanquishing the very idea of will with something else, and that something is intellect—again, capitalized. "If Intellect and Will be compared to one another," he writes, "according to the universality of their respective objects," that is, what each leads to, "then . . . the Intellect is absolutely higher and nobler than the Will." To Aquinas, Will represents man's urge to break free from the constraints of duty to God and duty to Christendom. Intellect is the path, for Thomas, to communion with and dedication to those highest qualities of the good. Man must think to find God, not act. Aquinas calls for a meditative stillness of communion. Man's duty for Thomas is a duty to *be*—which we might see as duty to *think*, thus his emphasis on the Intellect— rather than a duty to act. Action distracts from godliness.

The good Thomist is in a sense a man who is still; he is not acting but only reflecting on the essential qualities of God's creation. By extension, the good Christian state for Aquinas, much as for Cicero, is the state in its proper alignment with God's will, and more or less still. Justice for Cicero, the stoic, is about not doing, about rejection of the appetite. And so it is too for Aquinas.

Thus it is no surprise that when Aquinas begins to work through Augustine's various writings about war and distill from them a three-part test for the Just War, the theme that emerges is one of obedience. Where the tribal image of war is that of a good man throwing himself into battle, and the modern image of war is of a state mobilizing its troops in order to reach a larger political goal, Aquinas presents an image somewhere in between the two. The essential motive to fight for Gilgamesh, for the Greek soldier at Troy, for the Sioux warrior at Little Big Horn, or for the medieval Muslim soldier depicted by Ibn Kahldun was honor, a personal motive. The essential motive for the modern war-making machine of the state—for the massed troops of Woodrow Wilson in the First World War, for Churchill's soldiers in the Second, for the dog soldiers in Vietnam mobilized by Kennedy and Johnson and Nixon, or for American tanks in the sands of the Gulf War—is geopolitical: redraw a border, change a regime, stop the dominoes from falling, restore a vanquished state. But the motive force for Aquinas is neither honor nor politics but obedience: he casts Augustine's ideas about war so that they serve the interests of individuals as well as the state, individuals seeking most of all to get right with God rather than to prove themselves as soldiers and men or to do the business of a state with a large appetite or agenda.

Although the Thomist sense of the good moral life is seen by many today as pinched and narrow, nevertheless the philosophy of war that Aquinas codifies is one that for the first time seems genuinely about moral principles, and not at all about the glory of any man or the appetite of any state. So Aquinas stands as a tall figure in the history of Just War thinking, one who seems freest of compromise in his moral thinking as he tells his readers when they may undertake the bitter business of war for the sake of higher ideals. Although Aquinas is in the last analysis a somewhat frightening figure because the specific moral standards he has in mind are harsh and unforgiving, nevertheless there is a purity of method that many find appealing and long overdue in the history of Just War thinking by the time he takes pen to paper.

Yet the counterposition to Aquinas's is that no one is more cruel than the moral purist—and that no war is more prolonged and ugly than the war fought over virtue rather than over material interest. This needs to be borne in mind.

## THE THREE TESTS OF A JUST WAR
## FOR THOMAS AQUINAS

The first of the three tests of a Just War that Aquinas offers is that it be led by a "sovereign by whose command the war is to be waged." The word sovereign is a considered choice. Its meaning blends ultimate civil authority with divine sanction, invoking images of the pope's hand on the crown of Charlemagne or Napoleon. The second is that "a just cause is required, namely that those who are attacked, should be attacked because they deserve on account of some fault." Here Aquinas does not sanction attack because of some action undertaken by those to be attacked. Instead he says that they may be assaulted in battle because of some fault, some quality of their constitution, of who they are rather than what they have done. (If we wish to read "fault" broadly, to include bad action as fault, nevertheless Aquinas is talking here about what that action reveals about the actor's character.) Finally, Aquinas says that "it is necessary that the belligerents should have a rightful intention, so that they intend the advancement of good, or the avoidance of evil."

In all three cases, these criteria beg the question of higher authority: Who is to judge the faults of the nation we might attack? Who is to judge the rightness of our cause? Who is to judge the soundness of our sovereign? There is only one answer:

God. So for Aquinas, making war justly is an exercise in obedience to God. It is about the soldier's duty to the sovereign, and the sovereign's duty to God. (The next question that a modern reader is likely to ask—How can we know God's will?—does not enter into the Thomist view of war.) Where Augustine was ahead of his time in talking about peace as the ultimate end of war, Aquinas—particularly as his teachings reverberate in today's world—is something of an anchor in the evolutionary sea: he draws us back and holds us in place. He is ultimately a fundamentalist, and his interpretation of Augustine pulls the more ancient and more creative thinker toward the narrowness of the Thomist world.

Born in the early thirteenth century, Aquinas was witness to a period of remarkable corruption in the Catholic church but was by all accounts a devoted and principled student and scholar. His family tried to draw him away from church life when he was young, but he resisted the various temptations they placed in his path, among them a brief imprisonment by his brothers that culminated in an encounter with a prostitute (the brothers were sure she would be his monastic undoing; instead he sent her away). These stories of Aquinas's personal life fit his underlying view of man's relation to truth. Getting to God, for Thomas, was getting back to God, not going forward to God. His *Summa Theologica* has as its aim the collection of all the right answers to all questions, and in its very structure it offers a model for the finding of truth: answers are found by consultation, by review, by reflection. Not by action. Not by intellectual creation. Creation is God's work, and already done. Man is thus at best a reflective agent but not a creative one.

The twentieth-century philosopher Hannah Arendt, writing about Aquinas and Augustine in her book *The Life of the Mind,* sets the two in a kind of dialogue, with Augustine responding to Aquinas, though dead eight hundred years. Arendt likes to put the two together because she sees Augustine as before Aquinas chronologically but also ahead of him philosophically; in fact she sees Augustine directly answering Aquinas's objections to will. Augustine's answer, as Arendt sees it, is to transform Will into Love. For Augustine, Arendt wrote, "The transformation of Will into Love . . . was at least partly inspired by a more radical separation of the Will from appetites and desires. . . . Love could be invoked to redeem the Will because it is still active, though without restlessness, neither pursuing an end nor afraid of losing it." This notion of Love as a kind of Will-without-appetite reflects something Arendt sees in Augustine's ideal of the state: a state neither in motion as an empire nor afraid to rule. Not driven but not timid; not afraid of the future or the larger world, but not out to evangelize or conquer them. This ideal state is as much a creation of Arendt answering Augustine's moral challenges with her own interpretation of Augustine as it is a clear expression of Augustine's own ideas. Indeed, part of the power of Augustine's ideas about the state is that they allow for a wider range of interpretation and application than most other early church voices. Similarly, Augustine's central ideas about what makes for Just War allow for broad application and make room for him as a champion of any number of widely ranging (and even contradictory) contemporary positions about war. At their worst, the Just War criteria that have their root in Augustine's writings can be used as excuses for war on behalf of a state (a plausible interpretation of Augustine's personal circumstance) or as aggressive tools of crusading armies of conversion (shedding the least kind light on Aquinas). At best, though, those criteria offer tools for saying no to an emperor bent on war, and for mobilizing an army to aid a stricken third party in need of defense—the highest good for which to make war, according to Augustine. And, as interpreted by Aquinas, those criteria lead firmly into the realm of moral motives, and quite explicitly reject the compromises of serving any king's court.

Thus Arendt sees Augustine as presenting a powerfully humanistic philosophy of moral duty, one driven by love, and she sees Aquinas coming along to restrict that vision, and to place it in the service of a harsh, church-bound morality. She sees that notion of love in Augustine as the secret to his appeal to modern thinkers, the root of the common practice of calling the most hopeful and tolerant views of Christian inspiration "Augustinian piety." For Arendt, it is love that makes Augustine modern.

Arendt, a Jewish survivor of Hitler's Germany, relies on that kind of love for humanity for her own vision of a more just world. Hardly a pacifist, she lived for a time in refugee camps in France before making transit to the United States. She easily conjures in her writings the image of the innocent man or woman behind barbed wire, looking past the men who enforce the horror of imprisonment, abuse, and even genocide to those who might raise their arms and say No, say Stop, and go as far as to make war for the sake of the innocent who suffer. That highest Augustinian ideal of Just War is something Arendt feels vitally. Yet she reaches further in her writings to understand the moral nature of the individual, particularly the accomplice to evil.

In her book *Eichmann in Jerusalem*, Arendt describes the trial of Adolf Eichmann, a mid-level Nazi functionary responsible for the transport of Jews from Poland and Hungary to the death camps. Eichmann had escaped Germany and made his way to South America after the Nazi state collapsed. Captured by Israeli agents in 1960, he was spirited off to Israel to face a trial for crimes against humanity. Arendt describes the fury of the Israeli people, many of them European survivors of the Holocaust, as they confront Eichmann. He becomes their symbol of the evil of Nazism, captured and held at their mercy, a living bit of the very substance of evil now held in their grasp as they prepare to destroy it. But Arendt sees something different. She sees Eichmann not as an active force of evil but as a passive player in an evil game, a pawn. Indeed, a conformist. She quotes Eichmann as saying that he could not succeed in business because he was too much an idealist, too hungry to be part of a greater cause, an instrument of great ideas. Her Eichmann is shallow, childlike, and entirely unable to think original thoughts. He lives in the world of the cliché, of the commonly accepted and collectively held preconceptions of the world. Eichmann's idealism was of a particular type—unreflective. Where the people of Israel, and much of the rest of the world, saw Eichmann as a vessel filled with evil, Arendt saw him as a vessel empty of real human substance. He could not act morally, she thought, because he could not think independently or reflectively. He could do only what he was told; he could not say no. He was, Arendt wrote, all too typical of most people, going about his life avoiding conflict and doing what—anything—he was asked to do by his social superiors. Thus her book's full title: *Eichmann in Jerusalem: A Report on the Banality of Evil.*

Hannah Arendt's analysis of Eichmann parallels the theological debate on the nature of evil between the Manichean and the Augustinian views. Mani, a third-century figure on the fringe of the Christian world, viewed evil as an active presence that needed to be battled and destroyed. Augustine, in contrast, saw evil as the absence of good rather than as the presence of a substantial force. In the face of evil, the Manichean seeks to destroy what he beholds. The Augustinian seeks to change it—to love it, to introduce it to grace. Arendt takes from the story of Eichmann the idea of a high civic obligation to teach the habits of reflective thought, to emphasize positive early social action in a cycle of events that might otherwise lead to war. Her notion of Augustinian love becomes an argument for the kind of aid-and-education response to crisis that has become second nature to Western nations and the nongovernmental organizations that operate within them. That abstract argument she framed between Augustine and Aquinas, the argument about Will, Intellect, and Love, becomes real in the larger social context of world affairs in the decades following the fall of Nazi Germany and the hanging of Eichmann in Israel.

Yet Augustine was not a modern thinker by any measure, nor was he living in an era of the state as we understand it today. The important difference—the gap that cannot be bridged—between Augustine's idealism in *City of God* and the idealism of the earliest thinkers who truly belong in the modern tradition is that Augustine, especially in *City of God*, is a defender of the status quo. To the extent that he was inspiring people to think of new possibilities, those possibilities were still essentially spiritual, matters of belief and feeling that were not meant to connect to civic action but only to civic satisfaction. Hannah Arendt states plainly the profound difference between the Augustinian innovations of thought and those of later thinkers who said similar things about man's spiritual worth but connected those observations with a call to civic action: "The interconnected ideas of Mankind AND Progress came to the foreground of philosophical speculations only after the French Revolution had demonstrated to the minds of the most thoughtful spectators the possible actualizations of such invisibles as *liberté, fraternité, egalité,* and thus seemed to constitute a tangible refutation of the oldest conviction of thinking men, to wit, that the ups and downs of history and the ever-changing affairs of men are not worth serious consideration."

## HISTORY'S FAILURE TO STAND STILL

History ultimately rejected Augustine and Aquinas by failing to stand still—by failing to preserve the Holy Roman Empire, and by failing to bring the greatest rewards to the most pious civic bodies, those that looked inward, rejecting will and relying instead on intellect. But when history rejects an Augustine and an Aquinas—when it looks not inward and backward for truth but outward and forward, not only to God but to the world and works of men—who takes the place of Augustine, Aquinas, and their clerical brethren as a source of fundamental guidance for thinking about war? Who becomes interested in these ideas about the nature of history and the affairs of men if the churchmen are not entirely adequate to the task? Arendt had a clear answer on the broader issues: the philosophical architects of the age of revolution and the thinkers who followed them. As for questions of war, her general guidance, refined to the particular purposes of Just War thinking, brings us back to Rousseau, Kant, and Locke, and then quite directly back, once again, to Clausewitz and Hegel. Rousseau, Kant, and Locke were essential to the question of what the state could and should be. But Clausewitz and Hegel, writing after the ideas of these three earlier thinkers had set the world on fire, were able to look at the new states emerging and consider not only what those states *were* but what in fact those states *wanted*. That is to say, Clausewitz and Hegel take up the question of will once more, but in a world radically different from what Aquinas could have imagined.

When the idea of the will of the state reemerges with Clausewitz and Hegel, it has little to do with God and much to do with the state as a force, a modern creature that relies on the works of men but draws them into a collectivity always in motion, organizing and directing human aspiration. These thinkers have much in common with Machiavelli, but their stage is the planet, not the court, their arbiters not princes and kings but abstract notions of power, reach, and efficiency that become more vividly clear in the modern culture of globalization for which their ideas laid the foundation.

In his book *On War*, Clausewitz sets the stage for his discussion of war by asserting something that seems to personalize war and reflect its classical, tribal roots: "War is nothing," he writes, "but a duel on a large scale. Countless duels go to make up war, but a picture of it as a whole can be formed by imagining a pair of wrestlers. Each tries through physical force to compel the other to do his will. . . . *War is thus an act of force to compel our enemy to do our will.*" So, does Clausewitz see war as the struggle of men? Not really. War is a duel, he says, and a wrestling match, but notice that he is conflating all actions in a given war into one duel, one wrestling match. War is not two men fighting; war is *like* two men fighting. It is not the act of individual men, it is the fact of states acting like men. Specifically, it is states acting with the appetites of men, the will of men. The players are abstract forces playing the warrior role once played by individuals. "Combat in war," he writes, "is not a contest between individuals. It is a whole made up of many parts. . . ." Where an older view of war saw that a man's character was revealed in battle, Clausewitz says the same about the state: "War is an instrument of policy," he writes. "It must necessarily bear the character of policy and measure by its standards. The conduct of war, in its great outlines, is . . . policy itself, which takes up the sword in place of the pen. . . ." Again, Clausewitz leads us back to the fundamental question: Given that we are talking about state action when we talk about war, how does a state act morally?

Christian Just War doctrine offers only a partial answer, because the strand of Just War thinking that began with Augustine—centered on Augustine's paradoxical statement that the purpose of war is peace—was compromised even as it was uttered. Just War theory emerged as a kind of apologetics, in part because Christian Just War doctrine frames questions about war more than it provides answers to those questions. Only when the center of Just War thinking breaks away from state religion can it regain its usefulness as a balance against necessary state action rather than a justification of it. That did indeed happen, in the work of the writers, thinkers, and revolutionaries who created the European Enlightenment, beginning with Rousseau, extending through Kant and Jefferson and eventually to Hegel and Clausewitz. Yet the church was not removed from Just War tradition. Instead its role and its teachings were greatly changed. Those changes were on dramatic display in the Catholic Just War teachings of the twentieth century.

# 3

# THE CATHOLIC VOCABULARY OF WAR: THE CENTER AND THE FRINGE OF CATHOLIC JUST WAR DOCTRINE

IN 1983 the Conference of Catholic Bishops in the United States issued a "Pastoral Letter on War and Peace." The letter made news because it talked directly about the use of nuclear weapons and took a stand against the nuclear arms race. It said specifically that the intentional destruction of cities and civilian populations in war was never just, and it seemed to condemn the U.S. nuclear attacks on Hiroshima and Nagasaki that had occurred at the end of the Second World War. Coming as it did while Ronald Reagan was in the White House and Soviet rule firmly entrenched in Moscow and throughout Eastern Europe, the pastoral letter was clearly intended to offer guidance for American Catholics in the nuclear age. It saw the nuclear arms race as "one of the greatest curses on the human race; it is to be condemned as danger, an act of aggression against the poor, and a folly which does not provide the security it promises."

But the pastoral letter did more than address nuclear weapons. The bishops, speaking as "moral teachers," also laid out the principles of a modern Catholic Just War doctrine, drawing from church law, from Augustine and Aquinas, and from secular Just War traditions as well. "Catholic teaching begins in every case with a presumption against war," they wrote. But "every nation has a right and duty to defend itself against unjust aggression." The bishops wrote plainly that "Offensive war of any kind is not morally justifiable." They also paid particular attention to the principles of "proportionality" and of distinguishing between soldiers and civilians.

Nine years later, Pope John Paul II formally issued the new catechism of the Catholic church, a comprehensive enumeration of all church teachings. The catechism prefaces its direct discussion of Just War principles with this remarkable statement: "Peace is not merely the absence of war, and it is not limited to maintaining a balance of powers between adversaries. Peace cannot be attained on earth without safeguarding the good of persons, free communication among men, respect for the dignity of persons and peoples, and the assiduous practice of fraternity." Defined so broadly, peace is obviously rare.

The power of this definition of peace is clear when applied to specific cases, ranging from Neville Chamberlain's situation in 1938 to George W. Bush's in 2003. The argument for Chamberlain's inaction in response to Hitler, and against Bush's obvious impatience to make war against Iraq in 2002 and 2003, is that peace is always preferable to war. By the standards of the 1992 catechism, though, Hitler's Germany and Saddam's Iraq were not at peace even when other nations were holding their own armies in reserve. Thus the test of making war against them is not the test of bringing war to a place at peace, but the test of weighing in, of taking a side, in a conflict already begun even if that conflict was not yet, or not still, a conflict of arms.

In the catechism, the first explicit criterion for *jus ad bellum*—the choice to make war—is last resort: "as long as the danger of war persists and there is no international power with the necessary competence and power, governments cannot be denied the right of lawful self-defense, once all peace efforts have failed." The influence of Cicero is clear here, with the idea of "peace efforts" and formal diplomacy obviously so central. Grotius is also in evidence, with the reference to international authority. The church tips its hat to the Rights of Man thinking of the eighteenth century as well, with the reference to the "goods of persons" and an allusion to the French Revolution ringing in the word "fraternity."

Less explicit but also clearly present is the limitation of Just Wars to wars of self-defense. The turn since the ages of Augustine and Aquinas is distinct: aid to innocent third parties is no longer the highest good in questions of war. The brave definition of peace is as close as the new catechism will come to suggesting that a nation's self-defense might not be the only—or best—justification for war.

The second explicit criterion for a Just War is that "the damage inflicted by the aggressor on the nation or community of nations must be lasting, grave, and certain." This is a remarkably high standard; it would not allow, for example, a war against a nation that undertook violent raids of modest consequence against another nation's homeland. It would also rule out the kind of war of disarmament in Iraq that President Bush spent much of 2002 preparing for, and which became a reality in 2003 (though many would disagree that the war in fact turned out to be the war of disarmament that President Bush had advocated and advertised).

The third criterion recapitulates the last-resort standard: "all other means of putting an end to it must have been shown to be impractical or ineffective."

The fourth criterion is that "there must be serious prospects of success."

The fifth and final criterion is proportionality: "the use of arms must not produce evils and disorders graver than the evil to be eliminated. The power of modern means of destruction weighs very heavily in evaluating this condition."

The catechism goes on to say that "the Church and human reason both assert the permanent validity of the moral law during armed conflict," or *jus in bello*. Specifically, "non-combatants, wounded soldiers, and prisoners must be respected and treated humanely." Then follows a statement that could have been written by Grotius himself: "Actions contrary to the law of nations and to its universal principles are crimes, as are the orders that command such actions." Unlike Grotius, the catechism does not attempt to define this "law of nations." It leaves the reader with the demand to be good and the nation with the demand to be decent, but it leaves most of the specifics largely undefined. Thus Catholic Just War doctrine continues to deliver a moral challenge but not a set of instructions. And the catechism is quite conscious of this fact. "The evaluation of these conditions for moral legitimacy belongs to the prudential judgment of those who have responsibility for the common good." The catechism offers a decisive statement of church teaching, yet prudential judgment remains a step beyond these teachings, and in this case, prudential judgment is all.

## ALL HUMAN LIFE IS EQUALLY PRECIOUS

The evolution of Catholic Just War doctrine, from Augustine to Aquinas to John Paul II, is a testament to the increasing distaste for war (certainly the new catechism will not call wars waged by Christians "peaceful pursuits"). An important point of progress in this evolution was reached in the mid-sixteenth century with the dramatic expansion of the Catholic church.

At the beginning of the Age of Discovery, the Catholic priest Bartolomé de Las Casas wrote his *Brief Account of the Devastation of the Indies* (1542), serving a similar relation to Columbus that Grotius served to Martin Luther—trimming the ugliest aspects of a great thinker's work away from his legacy. Las Casas essentially invented the anti-colonialist sensibility, noting from its very first acts that the Spanish colonization of the New World in the name of Christ brought more suffering than salvation to the Indian people. Las Casas said plainly that the exploitation of natives was wrong, that slavery was wrong, and that war motivated by religion was, flatly, wrong.

Where the tribal sense of war saw war's glory in terms of individual experience, Las Casas rediscovered the tribal perspective with a modern slant: the individual as *object* of war, not subject. As one of the first participant-observers, a proto-anthropologist, Las Casas framed the moral experience of war in terms of innocence rather than action, and in terms of war's arrival from abroad rather than the journey out to war. In doing so, he rejected the group-level perspective of the conqueror—in the name of Spain, in the name of Christendom, or in the name of civilization—and set forth instead the individualization of the assaulted, the invaded, the primitive.

He chose to see not the *glories* of war but the *tragedy* of war in personal terms. The new Catholic catechism reflects this spirit clearly. "Because of the evils and injustice that accompany all war," the catechism says, "the Church insistently urges everyone to prayer and to action so that the divine goodness may free us from the ancient bondage of war." All wars bring sin—no war can be a peaceful pursuit. The 1992 catechism teaches lessons that the Roman Christians simply did not, lessons that the prevailing powers within the church did not embrace for centuries after the fall of Rome. Las Casas showed deep courage in writing against the interests of empire and of his church, which in the sixteenth century sat beside the king of Spain much as Augustine had sat beside Constantine of Rome. Yet what began as dissent for Las Casas has become a central tenet of church teaching today.

## "SHARP WARS ARE BRIEF"

Of the Catholic Just War criteria, one, the likelihood of success, has become a compelling point of interest in the past few years. Following America's policies of managed warfare in Korea and Vietnam, and the degrees of stalemate and defeat they produced, we have seen emerge in the United States what is now called the "Powell Doctrine"—when we fight, we fight with overwhelming force to ensure a quick and decisive victory. Thus Robert P. George, the McCormick Professor of Jurisprudence at Princeton, has written that "Our leaders are, in my judgment, morally obligated to use as much force as necessary, subject to the principles of just warfare, to protect innocent Americans and other potential victims of terrorism. It would be an injustice for them to fail to employ the necessary force."

We can take this notion of overwhelming force for granted, as an obvious—perhaps even the only obvious—approach to making war infrequent by making the wars we engage in fast and decisive. Yet the "low-intensity conflict" or "managed war" philosophy was itself part of a moral response to the First and Second world wars, wars that were vastly more pervasive in their effects, in particular their damage to the civilian populations they were fought among. The men who managed the U.S. military during the Korean and Vietnam wars were mostly veterans of the Second World War. Their tactical restraint had many sources, ranging from the legalistic constraints of the international institutions created in the wake of the Second World War, to their faith in technologies that held exaggerated promise to limit the destruction of war, particularly to civilians, while accomplishing war's aims. But we cannot too quickly dismiss the fact that many of these men had lived on the battlefields of Europe and Africa during their own years as dog soldiers, and had a genuine personal revulsion to the effects of the total war they had seen. These three forces—an almost sentimental moral revulsion to the effects of total war, faith in the growing technologies of the 1950s and 1960s, and the inevitable middle-roadism of consensus politicking within institutions like the United Nations and NATO—created a worldview that made managed war seem not only inevitable but enlightened.

In contrast, the idea at the center of the Powell Doctrine is not a new one, but it was well suited to the moment of the Gulf

The fighting had begun at the urging of Slobodan
a former Communist apparatchik under Yugoslavian
Marshal Tito, who saw a path to power in an appeal
hatred as the central Yugoslavian state deteriorated.
the lead of Franjo Tudjman, the somewhat less geno-
equally chauvinistic leader of the breakaway ex-
n state of Croatia, Milosevic led an irregular army of
campaign of ethnic cleansing in and around the Ser-
ation centers in the Yugoslavian countryside, and in a
ult on Muslim civilians in the multiethnic capital of
After years of tepid response from the UN and West-
s, by 1993 a consensus was building that more forceful
s needed to keep the growing war from spreading
ard Greece and north toward Hungary. The unhappy
ong many Western leaders was that sides needed to
. The Muslims of Bosnia—along with a small but visi-
ce of other Croats and Serbs who embraced the cos-
ethic of the infant Bosnian state, formed under fire
ored by a declaration of rights modeled on the U.S.
on—made a loud and steady appeal: we are being de-
a civilian population.

osnian Muslims seemed to the world to be the inno-
. Western airways were filled with images of Serbian
ng on the marketplaces and apartment buildings of
and of detention camps housing sometimes skeletal
risoners leaning against barbed wire, evoking the con-
camps of the Second World War. The Croats seemed
categorize, and for the moment they were less the
the world's attention. Yet there was more to the prac-
lations of alliance.

e French in particular, a lingering memory of the

War. The critical factor that made it the right doctrine for that
war was the relative weakness of the armies of Iraq, which did
not fight as long or as fiercely as most observers had expected.
With an imbalance of power, the Powell Doctrine works in both
practical and moral terms. The inevitable outcome arrives
sooner, and the duration of war is shortened. But the closer we
come to equilibrium of forces, the uglier the attempt at overwhelming force becomes. Consider, for example, the American
Civil War.

In 1863, President Abraham Lincoln issued General Order
100, a detailed set of pronouncements about the conduct of war
prepared by a professor of history named Francis Lieber, then a
refugee for the second time, having come to the United States
from Germany, and then from a professorship at South Carolina
College north to Columbia University. Lieber had fought with
the Prussian army, likely within shouting distance more than
once of Carl von Clausewitz, and had been wounded in the battle against Napoleon at Waterloo. Lieber took a university degree from the university at Jena, the very town where Hegel
had hidden in a cellar while the Prussian army fought and lost
against the French. As an official American philosopher of war,
though, Lieber had less sympathy for the cellar-dwelling civilians than he might have, and some historians lay at his doorstep
the blame for Sherman's murderous march through the South.

In General Order 100, Lieber rejected the immunity of civilians that Grotius had so ably articulated three centuries earlier,
declaring instead that "the citizen or native of a hostile country
is . . . an enemy, as one of the constituents of the hostile state or
nation, and as such is subjected to the hardships of war." Those
hardships, in Lieber's view, included what modern military eu-
phemists call "collateral damage." Put more simply, Lieber en-

couraged the Union army to strike hard at any and every target, with minimal concern for civilians who might be harmed in the process. Why the lack of interest in a more measured approach to battle? "The more vigorously wars are pursued, the better it is for humanity. Sharp wars are brief." The Powell Doctrine would not be as explicit in its disregard for the welfare of civilians, and it would not be as brutally clear about the fate of enemy civilians in the face of an onslaught. But there is a shared spirit here between General Order 100 and the idea of overwhelming force applied sharply and without reservation. Sherman's march was an expression of Lieber's ideas, and while it would be unfair to call the Gulf War endgame an expression of Lieber's ideas, the image of an effective fighting force facing an opponent of rapidly diminishing ability on a plain of battle left littered with corpses, flattened buildings, and the remnants of a vanquished fighting force, is similar enough to the late stages of the Civil War.

So American history offers two divergent approaches to the idea of decency: wage war carefully—a multilateralist, humanitarian approach with all due attention paid to minimizing harm in every day of every battle; or wage war with overwhelming force, to make the process brutal, decisive, and brief, so that peace may be achieved sooner, even if on bloodier wings. The first of these alternatives is increasingly assumed to be the only decent approach in an age of international cooperation marked by the end of the cold war, a prolonged proliferation of on-the-ground missions undertaken by the United Nations, and the successful launch of the European Union. Yet war by its nature is about disagreement, not accord. To attempt to impose a structure of reason and cooperation on the most unreasonable and uncooperative of ventures can easily result in the manufac-

ture of a philosophy of war that is
than wars have known in the pas
worse for humanity because of that

The Catholic Just War criterio
pitches its tent right here, where li
with the lessening of restraint over
recent book about the war in Kos
its title: *Winning Ugly*. Particular
where regular military culture is ra
loyalties regularly, and to the exte
exists at all there is no distinction b
and military, overwhelming force
nage in the Afghanistani region of
not only images of collapsed cave
the entire topography of a region
bombing.

A case study in the attempt to
against decency in the specific act
resort test—is Bosnia. What looke
genocide caught the world's atten
lective will to *do something* was cle
Western nations, but the specific
what to aid the innocents of the f
subject of debate in any number o
of a great deal of moral posturing
the opinion pages of newspaper
globe.

The worst effects of the pr
seeking bureaucratic approach to
the "community of nations" are e
Plan, floated to short-circuit the g

Yugo
Milos
stron
to et
Follo
cidal
Yugo
Serbs
bian p
steady
Saraje
ern na
action
south
feeling
be cho
ble pro
mopol
and an
Consti
stroyed

The
cent pa
shells f
Sarajev
Muslim
centrati
harder
center
tical cal
For

fierce Serbian resistance to Hitler under the leadership of Tito, who eventually became Yugoslavia's postwar, Iron Curtain head of state, led to the false presumption of a certain amount of decency among the Serbs (though the story of the Serbs in the Second World War was yet more complex: many exposed to the new, post-Soviet Serbia often referred to its armed representatives as Chekists, emphasizing their likeness not to Tito's Serb partisans but to the fascist Serbs of the time, who fought Tito and the allies as a fifth column for Hitler, and were known as the Cheka).

For the Russians, the most salient facts were that Serbs were orthodox Christians and maintained cultural and ethnic ties to their own weakened post-Soviet state. Too, the Bosnians counted among their thin armed forces some number of anti-Western fundamentalist Islamic fighters, many of them veterans of the Afghan Mujahideen who had pushed the Soviets out of Afghanistan and were generally disposed to hate the Russians. With an ugly civil war taking shape in largely Muslim Chechnya, the Russians were entirely ready to see Bosnia as part of a larger Muslim conspiracy against Christian Europe.

And then there was the matter of long-simmering tension between Greece and Turkey, bitter enemies often tempted to take up arms themselves, a potential conflict of Orthodox Christian and Muslim states that could become cataclysmic.

England, France, and the Netherlands already had peace-keeping troops on the ground in the former Yugoslavia, through the UN. Widely believed to be ineffectual, these troops represented targets of the first order to the Serbs in the event of a visible Western alliance with the Bosnians. And they were scarcely beloved by the Bosnians themselves, who saw the powder-blue helmets of UN troops as symbols of the West's troubled conscience joined with an absent will. An arms embargo supported by the UN and NATO had the effect of limiting, at least to a degree, the risk to other European nations, and so the embargo was widely supported outside of Bosnia. Yet political geography meant that the arms embargo effectively cut off Bosnia from new arms while Serbia, the single most important trading partner with Romania, Bulgaria, and Estonia, and a trading partner of growing significance with Russia and the Ukraine, could continue to import arms through the porous borders to its north and east.

Within this fractured context, two senior Western diplomats, Cyrus Vance, former U.S. secretary of state, and David Owen, former British foreign secretary, put forth their plan.

The Vance-Owen Plan parceled the former Yugoslavia into ten federated provinces, three Serb, three Croat, three Muslim, and one mixed. It was the very structure of compromise, built of evenhandedness and structural fairness. Yet, like the UN-declared "safe havens" during the worst of the fighting—places the UN beseeched refugees to journey toward with the promise of safety; places that in at least two cases UN peacekeepers chose not to defend in the face of Serbian assault, resulting in the massacre of Muslim civilians by Serb forces—the ten cantons of the Vance-Owen Plan were perfect on paper, elegant even, but impossible in practice. The plan, the Center for Security Policy wrote in 1993, as the United States considered endorsing it, "unmistakably rewards Serbian aggression and legitimizes its systematic practice of genocide in territories seized by force." That is to say, compromise—indeed, peace itself—is not necessarily a good thing if such a peace ratifies the victory of unjust actors. This very prospect turns Augustine's notion—that the ultimate end of war is peace—toward its ugliest prospect.

And it affirms the 1992 Catholic catechism's view of peace as something greater than the absence of war. The unjust peace of "containment" that allows a murderous head of state sanction and even reward if he keeps his horror far enough from other nations' lands and quiet enough that it does not find its way to their television news shows, points to the unavoidable necessity of war at times. Better war than the peace of contained genocide; better war than peace with tyrants. Better war than the peace that is the highest good of the functionary. This is the peace that was the highest good of Neville Chamberlain, as it was the highest good of Vance and Owen, and as it remains the highest good of Senator Mitchell. Again, the Center for Security Policy, from 1993: The Vance-Owen Plan "equates those responsible for Serbia's crimes against humanity with the victims of those crimes. It would also seem to make moot the essential prosecution of those who also perpetuated such actions."

Yet we have seen just such prosecutions because the Vance-Owen Plan failed. Instead more fighting raged, and the United States eventually chose to risk the disillusion of its NATO partners and strike at the Serb communications infrastructure with a Tomahawk missile. That missile represented the willingness of the West to raise its collective sword, to stand ready to make war, to invoke Orwell. The American ambassador to Yugoslavia quietly encouraged the Croatian army, in an uneasy but effective alliance with the Bosnian forces, to use all the weapons it could find (which of course meant sanctioning violations of the nominal arms ban) and to press the Serbs on the battlefield, thus pulling back on the West's long-standing and well-intentioned pressure for Croatia to go slow. The Croats won battles, and the American ambassador, son of the economist John Kenneth Galbraith, nodded his approval. The Croats allowed shipments of arms from Iran through to the Bosnians, and Galbraith nodded approval. The Bosnians then began turning back Serb forces themselves.

Then, his forces weakened, Milosevic was called to Dayton, Ohio, to negotiate. The Vance-Owen Plan died. In its place, the Dayton Accords imposed a better vision—a stronger, more decent sense of what a just peace might mean following an unjust war. The Dayton Accords did what Vance-Owen centrally would not do: it took a side. Though Milosevic agreed to the accords, he did so under enormous pressure and after considerable military setbacks, once the Clinton administration made clear its support for Bosnia in many symbolic and practical ways. Still, the Dayton Accords were political at their essence, and they needed to recognize the competing interests of all parties, even those who had committed atrocities. Thus the postwar map of the former Yugoslavia that emerged from Dayton still had the strong color of compromise and convenience; nonetheless it took a position. Of the territory contested by the Serbs and the emerging state of Bosnia-Herzegovina, 49 percent would go to the Serbs and 51 percent to Bosnia-Herzegovina. Thus a good deal of real estate cleansed of Muslims would remain Muslim free, in effect institutionalizing practical victories for the forces of ethnic cleansing in many areas. Yet the winner, by a single percentage point, was Bosnia. The weight of the Western world came down—just barely—on the side of the Bosnian people and the Bosnian state. Finally there emerged that rarest quality of modern states at peace: moral judgment. Only that could begin the end of the war in the former Yugoslavia. And that, of course, is at the heart of Just War doctrine; indeed, it is where Just War thinking (the mere inclination to address the central questions of war from a moral perspective) and Just War philosophy (the habit of addressing these questions with some degree of structure over time) meet the practical world, emerging as practice and policy, and weighing against the inevitable interests of states to preserve the practical advantages of their own peace and enact a small degree of justice. It is rare enough to see this happen, but in the case of Bosnia, the genocide that was halted and the slogan "Never again" seemed to have some relevance and even some power.

## IN GEORGE H. W. BUSH'S POCKET

Among American military intellectuals—particularly among those few who spend time at conferences that take up issues of Just War philosophy—a story about President George H. W. Bush circulates. The president, the story goes, had an aide who had been a serious student of religion before becoming a naval officer (I first heard this story from a naval officer; I suspect that air force officers make the protagonist an air force intellectual, that army intellectuals make the hero an army officer, and that Marines would deny the story entirely). As the Gulf War was heating up, the president asked this aide to write out, on a small card that might fit in the president's pocket, the essential principles of Christian Just War doctrine. The aide complied, and the president went through the Gulf War with Just War doctrine in his pocket.

Whether or not this story is true, I believe it is told to make a few points. First, that the elder President Bush was reflective and informed about the moral challenges of waging war. Second, that the American military establishment has significant moral and intellectual resources, and that these resources play an active role in the culture of military policy. And finally, that mere proximity to Just War thinking is a moral plus and makes wars better. From this last perspective, Christian Just War doctrine being in the president's pocket begins to seem like less than a good thing for the Christians. Although many Americans once famously worried that the pope would have President Kennedy in his papal pocket, now Christians—Christian pacifists most particularly—might be forgiven for their concern that their own thinkers are in the American president's pocket.

The greatest moral challenge to Just War doctrine in each great religious tradition is proximity to the state's appetite for war. Consider, for example, the image of Napoleon being crowned by the pope.

For his coronation in December 1804, Napoleon had overruled his advisers when they suggested he stage the event along the Champs du Mars, the broad strip of park that today lays between the Ecole Militaire and the Eiffel Tower. The invocation of Mars, the god of war, might have seemed appropriate for a man who had turned the people's revolution of France into a platform for his own coronation as the new hereditary emperor. But Napoleon chose instead to be crowned inside the cathedral of Notre Dame. The pope came from Rome to preside. Napoleon orchestrated the moment of coronation so that the pope, seated, would hand the crown to the new emperor, who would stand and then place the crown on his own head. In David's painting *The Coronation of Napoleon I*, we see the crown on Napoleon's head, and in his hands a second crown that he is about to place on the head of his empress, Josephine. Napoleon holds the crown gingerly aloft, fully invested at that moment with the pope's blessing, and about to exercise the final act of his self-coronation, the spiritual power of church and state bound together. At that precise moment Napoleon had taken the pope's blessing and symbolically held it in his hands. The churchmen in the painting look in various directions with apprehension and resignation. The emperor's court—the various aides and lackeys—stand apart as the benefits of standing in Napoleon's shadow only increase. They look to Napoleon coyly, happily, and entirely in command. In this moment the state has taken the moral authority of the church and holds it firmly. The warrior king is no supplicant or student of the pope; rather, he reflects upon the possibilities that come from holding the word and will of the church in his own hands. This is the consequence of Christian Just War doctrine at its worst. Critics of the Catholic Just War tradition in particular can take some comfort in the more genuine bias against war that has become church doctrine under John Paul II, though the church continues to leave great moral latitude to the prudential judgment of those who govern, including, as always, true democrats and true tyrants.

This potential for the shallow justification of a ruler's martial intentions applies just as well to the Just War teachings of other religions. Both Augustine and Aquinas wrote as Christian leaders living within Christian nations. Without a Jewish state for almost two millennia, there were no Jewish wars that needed justifying or Jewish armies that needed restraining, and thus no doctrine clearly postulated to accomplish these things. Among the most compelling stories of religious teaching about Just War, however, is certainly the Muslim tradition of Jihad: communal self-defense and understanding of peace and the common good. It is part of a dramatic struggle under way today to define the center of Islam. Those who prefer to ignore it find themselves drawn in nonetheless.

# 4

# MUSLIM AND JEWISH
# JUST WAR TRADITIONS:
# THE CENTER AND
# THE FRINGE

*Every religion has its warrior face; we can choose to accept it, or reject it.*

Judaism, Christianity, and Islam share a common mythology, each tracing its origin to the story of Abraham. As the oldest of the three religions, Judaism in its core texts and traditions has little to say about Christianity and Islam. Christianity, which began as a sect of Judaism, is highly aware of Jewish history and religious tradition. Islam, the youngest of the three faiths, is conscious of both Judaism and Christianity from its earliest history. The Hebrew Bible is important to all three religions, but the more general innovation they share is that all three are text-based. The Hebrew Bible, the New Testament, and the Quran each play somewhat different respective roles in Judaism, Christianity, and Islam, but each is central to its faith. In this innovation lies the inevitable tension for each religion between the revisions and adaptations to a changing world that mark the center of each religion as it is practiced, and the fringe fundamentalism of those who point to their holy texts and declare them absolute and complete, and their teachings inviolable.

The scholar and writer Sidney Hyman has talked about the Hebrew Bible as the text of a tribal leadership enjoying its moment of power and accommodating the real challenges of governing. Thus its views on war are largely tactical and practical, with the broader philosophical content emerging between the lines and reflecting the concerns of a leadership class with something to lose. The Christians of the New Testament, on the other hand, were not a governing class but an administration-in-waiting, running for office. Thus the idealism and philosophical appeal, the big promises and poetic celebration of the abstract, the unempowered, and the impossible. The Muslims who wrote the Quran held a middle position, though even to use this phrase—"the Muslims who wrote the Quran"—is to pick a fight with the traditionalist view of the Muslim holy text. The Quran is seen by Muslims as the work of one man, the Prophet Muhammad. The words, in their original Arabic, were given to him in a revelation, through the frightening embrace of the angel Gabriel in a cave on Mount Hira. Over time Muhammad recited those words to followers who memorized them, and after his death scribes wrote them down (Muhammad himself, in the Muslim tradition, was a wealthy but illiterate merchant trader).

Islam was neither a ruling religion, like Judaism at the time of the assembly of the Hebrew Bible, nor an insurgent faith, like Christianity, viewed as a threat by a dominant power like Rome. Instead it was something new, built on a loosely assembled base of Jewish biblical traditions but radically remade in the image of the cosmopolitan trading culture of the Arab world in the seventh century. The Arab peoples, increasingly important as the centerpoint in world trade and the custodians of much of classical learning during Europe's dark ages, were an assembly of dozens and even hundreds of different city-states, tribes, and clans, without a common language, a common culture, or a common belief system. The traditions of the rest of the world touched the Arabs, but none were dominant. Within a hundred years of Muhammad's death, though, Islam had become a powerful organizing force. The legend of Muhammad himself sat at the center of Islam, represented in the book that was his legacy. It is no surprise, then, to find unity as one of the principal themes of the Quran. Its most practical commands deal with the very matters of community-building that helped establish the common identity of the Muslim world: the only language acceptable for prayer is Arabic, and so the many-tongued Arab peoples were given a common language; the central sin enumerated in the Quran is idolatry, and thus the central importance of one God was emphasized, without the distractions of saints, prophets, or other semi-divine creatures who might support factions or schisms; and, like the Christian New Testament— but not at all like the Hebrew Bible—the Quran foresees the creation of one single worldwide community of believers, the *umma*.

## IN THE BEGINNING

Just War philosophy in the Jewish, Christian, and Muslim traditions begins in the same place: the Hebrew Bible's Book of Deuteronomy, referred to in Hebrew as *Devarim*. Chapter 20 of the book begins this way: "When thou goest forth to battle against thine enemies, and seest horses, and chariots, and a people more than thou, thou shall not be afraid of them; for HaShem [literally "the name," and in this context God] thy God is with thee, who brought thee up out of the land of Egypt." A remarkable promise: God is on your side. This line of text—this promise—captures something ancient and unsettling, something present in our own time as it has always been. The prospect of armies battling, each persuaded that it alone holds God's favor, is the ultimate indictment of religion itself. Yet Deuteronomy only begins with this commonplace of collective spiritual self-satisfaction. As the text proceeds, it complicates the idea of having God on one's side, and it adds some important reservations and conditions to holding God's favor in battle.

Much of Deuteronomy's text on war concerns practical points. The question of who shall serve in the Jewish armies receives special attention "What man is there that hath built a new house, and hath not dedicated it?" the text asks, and then answers, "Let him go and return to his house, lest he die in the battle and another man dedicate it." But larger issues emerge soon enough. Forecasting Augustine's contradictory justification of war (the idea that the purpose of war is peace), Deuteronomy 20:10 reads, "When thou drawest nigh unto a city to fight against it, then proclaim peace unto it." But peace with conditions: if the offer of peace is accepted, "all the people that are found therein shall become tributary unto thee, and shall serve thee." If the offer is rejected, then the battle shall begin. And upon victory, "thou shalt smite every male thereof with the edge of the sword." But not the women, not the children, and not the cattle. These are to be the spoils of victory.

On the one hand, this injunction not to kill plays to the self-interest of the conquering army. The women will become concubines and wives, the children workers, and the cattle part of the Israeli herds. But a sense of decency pervades this bit of scripture as well. The women, children, and animals are not to be killed because it would not be right to kill them. A hint of the sanctification of all life—at least all life save the lives of men—certainly sits in this text. The humility and spiritual sense necessary even in battle are clearer a few lines later when the text commands that the conquering army of the people of Israel not destroy fruit trees as they loot enemy towns—a common practice of the time—"for is the tree of the field man, that it should be besieged of thee?" No, the reader is to understand, the tree has in some ways a higher status than man: it enjoys the innocence of God's creation, free of human sin. Particularly in light of tactical advantages gained by environmental destruction in modern wars—Saddam Hussein's burning of the Kuwaiti oil fields upon his army's retreat from that nation in 1991 is the obvious example—the awareness of the natural world's vulnerability in times of war is striking here.

But most of these concessions to decency, it turns out, apply all too narrowly. "Thus shalt thou do unto all the cities which are very far off from thee." But close by, in particular in the cities of the Hittites, the Amorites, the Canaanites, the Perizzites, the Hivites, and the Jebusites, "thou shalt save alive nothing that breatheth. . . ." Depending on the vagaries of interpretation, the fruit trees of the Hittites, the Amorites, and the rest, might be spared, but there are those who argue that these trees too are to be "utterly destroyed," like the men, women, children, and cows that live among them. Why the need for such brutality toward other cultures so close at hand? So that these others shall not set bad examples: "that they teach you not to do after all their abominations, which they have done unto their gods, so ye sin against HaShem your God."

The significance of this theme in the text is enormous. It suggests that moral thinking—including the entire Just War project—applies only when contemplating war against certain enemies. Against others, moral restraint is not a consideration. At the core of this principle is the idea that some people are not fully human, not the proper children of God.

A related story is told earlier in the Hebrew Bible, in the Book of Exodus. As Moses is leading the people of Israel through the desert after their escape from Egypt, during an especially trying period in which the Jews seem to be losing their faith in him, a grandson of Abraham, Amalek, attacks the Jews. Moses stands on a hill during the battle, holding his staff high. As long as his staff is raised, the Jews dominate the battle. As his arms tire and the staff lowers, the Amalekites rally and seem about to prevail. Finally Joshua, the Jewish warrior, and a companion hold Moses' arms high for him, the staff remains aloft, and Amalek is driven off. This is a heavily symbolic moment in the Hebrew Bible, and Amalek is often seen as a representation of the spiritual predators who come to a people of faith in their moments of honest doubt, to prey upon their natural skepticism toward their rightful leaders and profit from their uncertainty. After the battle, Moses is told by God that the Amalekites will thereafter hold a special place in Jewish thought: "Write this for a memorial in the book," God tells Moses, "and rehearse it in the ears of Joshua: for I will utterly blot out the remembrance of Amalek from under heaven." A few lines later, Moses says, "HaShem will have war with Amalek from generation to generation."

A look around Israel today finds no shortage of modern extremists who point to the Palestinian people and label them Canaanites or Amalekites. The intent is clear: set aside the decency and reflection demanded by the Hebrew biblical tradition of war, and "save nothing alive that breatheth. . . ."

In June 2002 *The Forward*, a national Jewish newspaper in the United States, printed a story with the headline "Top Lawyer Urges Death for Families of Bombers." It read, in part:

> A prominent Washington attorney and Jewish communal leader is calling for the execution of family members of suicide bombers.
>
> Nathan Lewin, an oft-mentioned candidate for a federal judgeship and legal advisor to several Orthodox organizations, told the *Forward* that such a policy would provide a much-needed deterrent against suicide attacks. . . . Lewin argued that the biblical injunction to destroy the ancient tribe of Amalek serves as a precedent in Judaism for taking measures that are "ordinarily unacceptable" in the face of a mortal threat. His proposal, however, was rejected by an Israeli diplomat in New York, and discounted, in terms ranging from mild to condemnatory, by a range of commentators, terrorism experts and Jewish communal leaders from across the American political spectrum.

This article makes clear the choice between center and fringe in all three religions that claim Abraham as their starting point.

Attorney Lewin is as true to traditional Jewish teachings as the parent who drags his child to a town square and stones him to death because he is disobedient (also called for in the Hebrew Bible), or a man who stands over his son in a public place, a knife to the boy's throat because he believes that God's voice is commanding, "Kill him," as Abraham believed.

The Hebrew Bible, particularly in Deuteronomy, is not shy about guiding the Jewish people into war. Yet the Bible does have its moderating moments, and as with the New Testament and the Quran, the book is comprehensive enough to support the old cliché that just about anyone can justify just about anything with a strong line of scripture. Yes, the Hebrew Bible is violent. It tells us at times to kill all the women and children and cows of our enemies. But it also presents a God who detests martial excess. King David, after all, was not allowed to build the great Temple of the Jews, we are told in Chronicles, because God declared to him that "Thou hast shed much blood upon the earth in my sight." And in Chapter 2 of Isaiah we are told that God's ideal is that warriors shall one day beat their swords into plowshares—a gentle vision of war's end, a just peace in which the strength of men is spent working the earth. But this vision comes only after these lines: "It shall come to pass in the end of days that the mountain of the Lord's house shall be established as the top of the mountains . . . and out of Zion shall go forth the law." So the end of war will come in the end of days, perhaps at the end of human history and certainly after a total victory by the Jews over other people's lands: thus out of Zion shall go forth the law.

If we value human civilization as it has unfolded in the centuries since the Hebrew Bible, the New Testament, and the Quran were written, we must take our sacred texts as starting points only, to be embraced in the context of the best that has been said and thought since. What does this mean for our understanding of war? It means that if we are to understand what these ancient faiths teach about war, what comes after the central sacred texts—the hundreds and thousands of years of interpretation, emendation, and outright revision—is as important, and in some cases more important, than the black-letter commandments of the Bible. Many will disagree and cling to the ancient texts in honest devotion. Others will seek to use the ancient texts as tools to diminish the experience and values of modern life, as weights on the scale of argument to overwhelm opposing opinion, or as cloaks to conceal prejudice, greed, and resentment.

Yet the distinction must be made between the fundamentalist who fashions his worldview from the words of the Bible and little or nothing else, and the follower of tradition who reveres the ancient text but also values the civilization built around that text. The former represents a fringe, always present though seldom of decisive influence in any of the three religions that begin their history with Abraham. The latter represents the most common, the most numerous, and the most enduring elements of each religion. It is to these thinkers, at the centers of their traditions, that we must look for Just War thinking. They can guide us with an eye toward preserving the achievements of men and women, of human civilization and culture, which those who begin and end with the scripture simply cannot do.

## THE TALMUD AND THE ORAL TORAH

In Judaism, the rabbinic tradition is particularly important. Traditional teaching holds that when Moses climbed Mount Sinai to receive the word of God, he was given two versions of the Torah: the ten commandments (from which flowed the five books that make up the Hebrew Bible) and what is referred to as "the oral Torah," teachings that go beyond the page and require the interpretation of rabbis for their full meaning. The very idea of the oral Torah creates special privilege and authority for the rabbi. Any Jewish man—and in some Jewish traditions, any Jewish woman—may study the Torah and other religious texts and become expert in Jewish ideas. But the rabbis have something more, something secret that only they know as keepers of the whispered knowledge given to Moses and passed from generation to generation among the rabbinate. Thus their decisions, their advice, and their worship all sit at a level slightly higher than that of other Jews. They know what others don't; debate can be pursued only so far; a challenge to a rabbi can be credible only to a point. The oral Torah trumps resistance and even doubt. It is a remarkable tool of religious authority.

The most coherent expression of Jewish Just War thinking after the age of the Hebrew Bible comes from Maimonides, the medieval Jewish philosopher who did more than any other commentator to make the *Mishneh*—the written essence of the oral Torah, recorded by rabbis after the fall of the Second Temple in 70 A.D—understandable to ordinary readers. Maimonides spelled out what he saw as the fundamental distinction in Jewish tradition between wars of obligation and optional wars. Wars of obligation, he wrote, were chiefly wars of self-defense and wars to reclaim traditional Jewish lands held by non-Jews. Optional wars were wars of empire, driven by desire for power and riches. Many interpreters of traditional Jewish philosophy say that optional wars are no longer possible; the fall of the Second Temple has meant that there is no longer a divinely ordained Jewish king, and only such a leader could prosecute wars of Jewish empire. Although this seems like a quibble—should the standards of what is right and wrong really depend on who sits on what throne?—it does bring traditional Jewish philosophy in line with the consensus of modern thinkers that wars of empire are simply wrong, that "optional" wars have no moral justification.

Still, the idea of the obligatory war remains troubling. It seems to require Jews—some say all Jews—to ensure that the biblical land of Israel is controlled by the current political state of Israel, above and beyond considerations of democracy, property rights, or other standards of decency. An extension of the principle of suspending the codes of Just War when facing the Canaanites, the Amalekites, and others, this traditional principle is hard to finesse. Traditional Jewish teachings do indeed say that the Jewish people are obligated to fight to dispossess people living in the biblical land of Israel, and if those people qualify as members of a few despised groups, to kill their children and their cows in the process. Certainly there is a strong parallel here to the Muslim idea of *dar al Islam*, the homeland of Muslim nations for which Muslim men are mandated to fight, even with the ugliest tools of war. But that offers little moral comfort. This biblical injunction and the Quranic injunction that sits beside it are simply contrary to any modern understanding of human rights and Just War. What is one to do with this?

What many modern Jewish interpreters do is to note the many contradictions in biblical teachings, emphasize the central moral teachings, and apply them in a way that forces a choice: refresh Jewish tradition, choose a nobler way, or accept the prison of the old texts and live lives bound up in innumerable contradictions and ancient prejudices. The choice, quite simply, is between the center and the fringe, between the dynamic view of a religion that can say, "This, here, is the true spirit of our belief, but that, there, is not," and the fundamentalism that declares, "We have no choice; we must do as we are told by the books written by our ancestors, for we are not made by God to think, simply to do."

## WAR AND PEACE IN THE QURAN

Like the Hebrew Bible, the Quran is not shy about bloodshed. Muhammad himself is portrayed as the leader of a massacre of the Jews of Khaybar in 628 A.D. Here the Jews are placed in a situation similar to that of the Amalekites in the Hebrew Bible: a people specifically targeted for annihilation. Yet there is a theme of peace and tolerance woven throughout the Quran, which says clearly that "Allah does not love aggressors."

But what is an aggressor? The ninth section of the Quran includes the command, "Believers, make war on the infidels who dwell around you, be firm with them." This too sounds a lot like the Hebrew Bible, though the Quran has followed the lead of the Christian New Testament and focused less on tribal identity, as the Hebrew Bible did, and more on belief. If the highest good in the Hebrew Bible was the survival of the Jewish *people*, and the highest good in the New Testament was the survival and spread of the Christian *idea*, the Quran rolls the two together—the highest good becomes the survival and spread of *communities of believers*. The tribalism of the Hebrew Bible is still with the Quran, but the tribe is not defined by blood or covenant, and the Chosen People idea has fallen away. As in Christianity, in Islam the idea of the faith is central, but as in Judaism, those who share it take on a special status.

Those outside the circle of the Christian idea in the New Testament are largely potential converts. In the Hebrew Bible, those outside the covenant are mostly bystanders, people who (if one believes the later commentaries) are bound by the seven laws that bear on gentiles rather than the 613 that bear on Jews, with the notable exception of those gentiles with an unhappy history involving Jewish real estate. In the Quran, those outside the circle of the Muslim idea have a chance to enter that circle, but much more is said about how to treat those who choose not to enter (fiercely) than about how to draw them in. The key word here is *infidel*. In the Hebrew Bible the hated Canaanites and the similarly despised Semitic tribes were finite in number; the rest of the world was split between largely neutral gentiles and the relatively small number of covenant-community Jews. In the New Testament, Christians are a small band but ready to expand exponentially: the world is their field of action, and an infinite number of new converts awaits. In the Quran, the largest mass of people fall into the category of "infidel," and that is the category that seems most ready for growth. To be an infidel is not at all a good thing in the Muslim vision of the Quran (9:121, "Believers, make war on the infidels . . .").

But where is the center of Islam and where is the fringe? This question is particularly vital in the wake of the September 11 attacks and the spread around the world of Osama bin Laden's violent interpretation of Islam's central teachings. Americans in particular are struggling to understand whether Islam is by its nature a religion of violence and conquest. If so, a violent posture toward Islam takes on the moral character of self-defense. If not, a more thoughtful and nuanced engagement with Islam—politically, socially, and intellectually as well as militarily—is absolutely necessary.

Ironically, bin Laden's view of Islam shares the most common shortcomings of the view of Islam held by many Americans: it is radically simplistic, and—more so in bin Laden's case but true enough throughout most of the United States—willfully ignorant of the range of rich traditions of Islamic thinking. That ignorance prevents otherwise well-intentioned thinkers and citizens from judging America's policies and predicaments intelligently. Certainly it prevents us from understanding not only the motives of the Muslim attackers but the disposition of the rest of the Muslim world. Further, that ignorance prevents us from forming appropriate motives of our own, in particular from distinguishing between our impulses toward self-defense and toward a military offensive.

The richness of Islamic history and thought begins to reveal itself in useful ways in the history of Islam after Muhammad.

## THE CHANGE IN ISLAM AFTER MUHAMMAD

One hundred and twenty years after the Prophet Muhammad's death, and as the Quran was beginning to reach masses of people within and outside Islam, political change began to sweep through the fast-growing Muslim empire. Muhammad's closest students and followers had become the rulers—the caliphs—of Arabia for a generation following his death in 632. In 661 a new movement took control of Muslim lands and extended the empire into India, Africa, and Spain. A civil war in 750 brought yet another radical political change to the empire. The new Abbasid dynasty, which ruled for five hundred years, encouraged debate of the Quran and the development of a code of laws based on the holy book, but apart from it as well, and open to change over time.

In the five hundred years of the Abbasid dynasty, who spoke for Islam? Many voices. The range of voices was itself a distinguishing characteristic of the era; it was an era that allowed debate.

No caliph's rule was absolute during the Abbasid dynasty. Factions were always breaking off from the mainstream, and the fundamentalist impulse was always present. A ninth-century Muslim legal scholar named Shafi was well known for his somewhat modern theory of judicial process that directly addressed the question of who spoke for Islam. Shafi proposed that in settling disputes, Muslim judges should look first to the Quran, and if that were not adequate, then to the sayings of Muhammad. If even the sayings did not provide sufficient guidance, the judges should seek a consensus among living scholars—and if they were not helpful, a judge might formulate his own ruling based on the closest precedent from other legal cases. The implications of this procedure were large: the Quran is fundamental, it suggests, but perhaps not enough, not complete. Perhaps it is only a beginning. The sayings of Muhammad, the consensus of scholars, the fact of legal precedent—all are voices to be placed in concert. *All speak for Islam.* The burden on the listener, then, is not so much to obey as to judge among competing claims for and interpretations of Islam's meaning.

In 820, while Shafi was speaking to an audience in Egypt, a group of fundamentalists rose from the crowd and killed him. Who speaks for Islam? Only one voice, his attackers' actions proposed. *And not your voice.* Thus the most basic distinction between center and fringe: the center contains and tolerates many voices; the fringe declares that only one voice may be heard. The center is open, at least to a degree; the fringe is closed.

Of the three religions that claim Abraham as their starting point, Islam is by design the least anchored in a central, mainstream version of itself. Roy Mottahedeh, a professor of religion at Harvard University, has said that "Islam is what every Muslim says it is. And it cannot be said often enough that there is no structure of religious authority in the Muslim community." The practical tools of religious and social authority central to Islam create no central church body, as the Catholic church does, and no key to biblical understanding that lives only with a specially empowered clerical class, as Judaism does through the oral Torah. Rather, Islam places more emphasis on the holy book itself to guide people. It leaves competing community-based power structures in the mosques. The Quran lays out a system and structure of belief that makes this so: there is no central adjudicator, no central interpreter of Islam's teachings. There is only the book; every other aspect of the religion is local. Thus the great irony that while in much of the West Islam appears to many people to have one face—the face of strangeness, of the Other—it is far more accurate to say of Islam than of Christianity or Judaism that it has *no* single face. Its singularity is entirely to be found in the holy book, the Arabic-language Quran. Again, Professor Mottahedeh: "Whereas Christians understand the great self-revelation or self-presencing of God to mankind to be in the birth of Jesus, for Muslims, that which God has sent to mankind is the Quran."

His is certainly not the only view. Many in the West struggle to find the "official" Islam so that they may make some sense of it. True, the history of Islam tells a coherent story, but it is as complex as the history of any enduring religious tradition. Thus the Christian evangelist minister Robert Morey, writing about the idea of Jihad, asks, "What if you meet a Muslim who denies that Islam teaches Jihad or who gives a novel interpretation of it? His personal opinion has no logical or legal bearing on what the religion of Islam officially teaches concerning Jihad. He may disagree with what Islam teaches, but this cannot alter the fact that Islam teaches it." So too we can say that Martin Luther broke the rules of official Christianity in his time, or fault Pope John Paul II's catechism because it cuts against the teachings of Thomas Aquinas. This is useful if one is making an argument, but it creates no understanding.

Over time, each religion has clearly seen itself shaped and re-shaped by the demands of civic life in a changing world. The center tends to be the form of religion that allows for its follow-ers to enjoy the greatest benefits (social, spiritual, and material) that each broader age allows. In part this is because those ver-sions of any faith that allow their followers to succeed according to the practical terms of the societies in which they live will have as partisans people who can get things done—people with ac-cess to the social and material tools of power. As they compete with other interpreters of their faith, these people will have ad-vantages that may seem almost unfair. The Judaism that says, in essence, go to work, succeed, participate in the broader profes-sional, social, and political lives of your nation, will have a great edge over the Judaism that says, in effect, stay home, stand apart, don't consort with people who are different. Thus in the never-ending contests within religions, the center exerts a kind of gravity that continually realigns the center of the faith with the practical demands of the larger world.

A less practical argument against fringe fundamentalism, is in a sense, a kind of fundamentalism itself. It relies on the holy book rather than the influence of civilization to make its case. Yet this kind of fundamentalism—perhaps it would be best called dynamic fundamentalism—pays special attention to the dynamic qualities of the holy book. It sees different voices, progressive change, and the essential qualities of elaboration, extension, and evolution of the faith *within* the holy book itself. It sees the holy book not as a simple, consistent statement capturing a static belief but as a captured image of years, decades, or even centuries in the life of an evolving faith.

Thus one answer to the question of why followers deviate from the literal word is that the holy text itself deviates from its own word: it contradicts itself, it evolves. And so one might say that the center of the Jewish faith is the understanding of Judaism that allows Jews to change their religion to roughly the same degree that it changes within the Hebrew Bible. The inner dynamism of the religion is recorded in the Hebrew Bible in the form of contradiction, variation, and evolution. Thus the static fundamentalist—the fundamentalist who pretends that the text is unchanging—reveals himself to be at the fringe, not at the center, because he rejects the hopefulness, the model and precedent for change, of the book itself.

The clearest example of these qualities comes at the very beginning of Genesis. In the first chapter of that book, God creates man and woman abstractly—the reader is told that "man and woman, he created them"—but not how. Then, in the next chapter, the creation story is told again, and differently. Here the reader sees God blowing the essence of life into the first man, whom God has formed of earth. Then the reader is told that God creates woman from the rib of man.

Why these two different tellings of the same story? Some scholars say that the Hebrew Bible is essentially an anthology, that two variants, written by different authors in different times, places, and styles, managed through a long editing process, likely spanning generations, to be included side by side. Scholars who are more theologically inclined talk about the humbling impact on the reader of a text that demands to be read differently from all other texts, beginning in its very first chapter. Neither of these views precludes the other, but both preclude the kind of static fundamentalism that says "obey the text," because the text is inherently—some would say intentionally—contradictory. It forces the reader to employ an interpretive lens, to choose some of the messages of the text and discard others. (If we do not discard some of the literal meaning of Genesis, we are left with two Adams, two Eves, two worlds, and perhaps even two Gods.)

## WHAT DO WE ASK OF THE HOLY BOOK?

In each religion, the holy book performs many tasks. Understanding what those tasks are, and are not, is central to defining where one fits in the structure of modern Judaism, modern Christianity, or modern Islam. In its earliest forms, the Hebrew Bible functioned as a receptacle of history for a powerful people who governed their own kingdom, recording laws and social codes along with that history. The New Testament functioned as a prophetic document, unveiling a new set of ideas and promising that all good things would come as those ideas spread throughout the world. The Quran created a common social, linguistic, and theological vision for a disparate people and brought into concert hundreds of tribes, sects, city-states, and small kingdoms to form, at first, a single but loosely confederated civilization, and two world-spanning empires over six hundred years. Secondary works of interpretation and expansion of the meaning of the Quran emerged in the centuries following, among them the works of eighth-century scholars who formulated Islamic law. Laws about highway robbery, called the *hirabah*, are particularly important to an understanding of the center of Islamic traditions about war and terrorism. These laws specifically forbade attacking people without warning, harming innocent travelers, and disrupting the ordinary workings of public life. They spoke to the dignity and decency of Muslim civilization and demanded a sense of honor and respect for life that could not tolerate terrorism of the kind that Osama bin Laden and others call for in the name of Islam.

Scholarly commentary on the Quran divided the world into the Muslim homelands, *dar al Islam*, and the remainder of the world, *dar al harb*, a vision similar to the structure supporting Jewish teachings about the difference between obligatory wars to protect Jewish homelands and optional wars of empire extending beyond the Jewish lands. The central character of the *dar al Islam* in traditional Muslim teaching is its peacefulness; the rest of the world is seen as a rudderless, unpredictable vessel, tearing itself apart to varying degrees. Protection of *dar al Islam* is of the highest importance, and virtually any means of fighting off invaders is accepted.

This view held the center of Islamic teachings until a few decades ago. In the 1960s, an era of decline and confusion in the Muslim worldview that had begun after the First World War seemed to be ending. A new era based on the enormous economic power of the oil being pumped from under Muslim sands was beginning. Wahba al Zoheli, a Sunni Islamic scholar of law and professor at the University of Damascus, was the leading voice in a movement of influential, mainstream Muslim scholars. He wrote about the idea of the *dar al ahd*, "the abode of the treaty," that would supersede the classical distinction between *dar al Islam* and *dar al harb*. With the advent of the United Nations, al Zoheli proposed to unify modern Muslim states under an internationalist umbrella. He argued for a Jihad of the spirit, as opposed to a Jihad of the sword, recasting the ancient Muslim call to arms as a call to spiritual reflection. With the great Muslim empire gone after a thousand years of world power, rather than accept a collective self-image of the defeated, al Zoheli proposed to see the end of empire as an opportunity to transcend the ugliness of conquest and empire, and claim a higher moral and civil status. Muslim nations would be the most forward-looking of all, the most willing to embrace internationalism in their civic lives while continuing whatever degree of Muslim piety they might choose in their homes and local communities.

Until 1980, when the Iranian revolution created a new image of the Muslim civic future—an image so different from the tolerant and cosmopolitan heights of the earlier Muslim empire—al Zoheli seemed to be pointing the way to a new Islamic political philosophy, reasserting Muslim culture as the most cosmopolitan and tolerant in the world, a status it held firmly in the age of the first great Muslim emperor, Saladin.

Saladin's era was one of great religious violence. A worldwide conspiracy to overthrow governments and kill large numbers of civilians in order to fulfill extremist religious prophecy was in progress throughout his lifetime. But the religious extremists of Saladin's age were not Muslims. They were Christians, and their violent means brought a great deal of martial success.

## SALADIN AND THE CRUSADERS

Saladin was born in 1138 in the city of Tikrit, now part of Iraq (and, in fact, the hometown of Saddam Hussein), in the midst of one of the great wars of civilizations, the Christian Crusades.

To understand the idea of the Crusades, Shakespeare is an excellent starting point. His play *Henry IV, Part 1*, opens with the English king anxious to mount an assault on what he calls the Holy Land, which the reader is to take as Jerusalem and its environs, then occupied by a remarkably diverse population. A civil war has kept Henry from his religious duty, but he thinks the time to take up the sword to defend Christ is at hand. "Friends," Henry says, "as far as to the sepulchre of Christ,/ Whose soldier now, under whose blessed cross/ We are impressed and engaged to fight,/ Forthwith a power of English shall we levy;/ Whose arms were moulded in their mothers' womb/ To chase these pagans in those holy fields/ Over whose acres walk'd those blessed feet/ Which fourteen hundred years ago were nail'd/ For our advantage on the bitter cross." A "power of English"—an army—will take to the roads and the seas and make their way south and east. And when they arrive, they shall kill Muslims (mostly) as well as some Jews and perhaps sundry others—Hindus, Pagans, even a few dark-skinned atheists. Why "chase these pagans in those holy fields"? Because there Christ's "blessed feet . . . were nailed . . . on a bitter cross." Fourteen hundred years is not long enough to exempt non-Christians from death for the crime of living where, according King Henry, they shouldn't.

The first of the Crusades began in 1095, and by 1099 European Christians had a tenuous hold on Jerusalem and other lands. They burned mosques and Jewish synagogues, and massacred civilian populations. For three hundred years, control of key territories shifted back and forth between Muslims, Europeans, and occasional opportunists unaffiliated with either force, while generation after generation of Crusaders persisted in their campaign.

In 1169, Saladin became the military ruler of large parts of Egypt and began a period of tolerance and civic openness in Cairo that expanded along with his empire. By 1174 he had conquered Damascus. By 1186 he had won parts of Iraq and Syria. And by 1187 he had extended his empire to include Jerusalem. In 1192 he signed a peace treaty with the English king Richard I—also known as Richard the Lionhearted—preserving his control over Jerusalem by allowing the Crusaders to take adjacent lands.

Saladin died a year later, and the tug of war over Jerusalem soon resumed. Saladin had studied Sunni theology before he joined the Egyptian army as a young man, and had had a reputation as a serious scholar. His understanding of Islam was a generous and tolerant understanding. He felt that his faith demanded respect for other faiths and civil regard for non-Muslims. Although the Christian Crusaders who came in wave after wave to take Jerusalem for their own prize regarded Muslims, Jews, and others as infidels, Saladin saw the Jews and Christians of his land not as infidels but as citizens and subjects worthy of his protection.

His relationship with King Richard has held the interest of European writers for centuries. Some ascribe Saladin's tolerance and civic decency to his brief contacts with the king. Others suggest that Richard spared Saladin and the civilians of Jerusalem only because the king fell ill and decided to return to

England. Jewish commentary on Saladin turns on one of the great cultural legacies of Saladin's rule: the enormously influential work of the Jewish scholar Maimonides, who himself had been a court physician to Saladin in Egypt.

Some scholars make much of the fact that Saladin was a Sunni Muslim, not a Shi'ite. Although it is difficult to weigh the importance of this distinction in any specific case, the difference between Shi'ites and Sunnis is generally important. Shi'ites make up a fairly small minority of Muslims in the world today, about 10 to 15 percent. Theologically they are more closely tied to the notion of divine civil authority than Sunni Muslims are. Shi'ites believe that the twelfth imam in the chain of succession from Muhammad is the only legitimate civic ruler of Muslim people and Muslim lands, and that until that twelfth imam appears, Muslim clerics ought to rule as deputies in his absence. The absent figure of the imam has become for Shi'ites a poetic representation of the absence of dominating power in the Muslim world, which has also disappeared.

While the foundation of Shi'ism is more mystical than other Muslim traditions, Shi'ites include the Ismaili sect, led today by the Aga Khan. Ismailis played an important role in preserving and transmitting classical Greek texts in the eighth, ninth, and tenth centuries, and rightly think of themselves as intellectually advanced and philosophically obligated to help others—beginning with their Muslim brothers—to a more nuanced understanding of the world. In particular, Ismailis train a great number of doctors and nurses in the Muslim world, and the Aga Khan has underwritten an enormous program to reform the universities of post-Soviet Central Asia, to bring what one might be tempted to call a Western-style, inquiry-based humanities education to countries like Tajikistan, Azerbaijan, and even corners of Russia. Ismailis will remind the Westerner who imagines the intellectual standards of Greece and Rome to be somehow beyond Muslims that it was Ismaili Muslims who brought the Greek classics to Europeans struggling to emerge from the Dark Ages. As European civilization crept back from those centuries of church-dominated ignorance, many Ismailis will say, Arab civilization was enjoying a cultural and material renaissance.

In contrast to the Shi'ite Muslim tradition, Sunni Islam is in theory more democratic. It is radically decentralized and encourages local control of the levers of religious and civic power. In some cases this means that local religious communities live more or less free from top-down civic governance. In others it means that local strongmen are not checked by the benevolent intercession of keepers of their faith's highest ideals. Today Sunni Islam includes a wide range of cultural and political practice. It is the umbrella for both the ecstatic and open Brotherhood of the Sufi and the tightly controlled and controlling Wahabbism of the Saudi kingdom.

Many Americans first heard the distinction between Shi'a and Sunni when the Ayatollah Khomeini came to power in 1980 in Iran. Khomeini's revolution was a Shi'ite revolution, and many Westerners mistakenly began to think of Shi'a as the revolutionary, anti-Western version of Islam, and Sunni Islam as somehow friendlier to the West. But that was scarcely the case.

The Sunni writer and activist Sayyid Abu'l-A'la Mawdudi is a giant figure in modern Islam, parallel to Turkey's secular leader Ataturk but pulling entirely in the opposite direction. Born in India in 1903, Mawdudi lived for a time in the Hindu city of Hyderabad. As a young man witness to the destruction of the Ottoman Empire, Mawdudi came to believe that the decline in

Muslim world power was a consequence of Muslim tolerance of infidels. In 1941, Mawdudi founded the Jumaat al-Islami party in Lahore, India. In 1947 the uneasy cohabitation of Muslims and Hindus in India ended abruptly with the independence of India from Great Britain. The bloody partition of Muslim Pakistan from Hindu India was to a small degree a triumph of Mawdudi's separatist ideals. But a homeland was not his principle desire; he wanted all the world to belong to Islam. The influence of revolutionary socialist and Communist ideals was peaking in the world as Mawdudi grew into adulthood, and his version of Islam clearly bears their imprint: "Islam is a revolutionary doctrine and system that overturns governments," he wrote. "It seeks to overturn the whole universal social order . . . and establish its structure anew. . . . Islam seeks the world. It is not satisfied by a piece of land but demands the whole universe." Mawdudi enjoyed his strongest following in Egypt, and his notions of Jihad as requiring "all forces and means" for an "all embracing revolution" has come, decades later, to justify suicide bombings and a broad range of attacks on civilians.

The Egyptian writer Sayyid Qutb was particularly influenced by Mawdudi. Qutb applied Mawdudi's example to Egypt, joining the violent Muslim Brotherhood and writing a series of books that drew upon the most violent and absolutist sections of the Quran to call for the violent overthrow of secular governments everywhere. Like Mawdudi, Qutb was influenced by revolutionary socialist and Communist ideas and took a "vanguard" approach to Islamic revolution. Rather than work with ordinary people to help them channel their energies toward revolution, he felt that a leading group of Islamic revolutionaries must overthrow their governments and impose total and strict Islamic rule on all the citizenry, with the intent to cultivate in them over time a desire for Islamic fundamentalism. This is very much the model of the routed Taliban in Afghanistan, today's radical Islamic government in Sudan, and any number of Islamic revolutionary forces from Lahore to London. But Qutb was not a man of parochial experience. He spent two years in the United States, shortly after the Second World War, living in Washington, D.C., Colorado, and California. That visit helped him add an informed anti-Western and anti-American element to his philosophy and indirectly helped fire the hatreds of Al Qaeda and other terrorist groups a generation later.

Qutb was executed by order of Egyptian president Nasser in 1966. In 1981 the Muslim Brotherhood—the organization Qutb had joined as a young man—assassinated Egyptian President Sadat as he sat reviewing a military parade of armaments largely financed by the United States.

It is easy to miss the model of civic Islam that Mawdudi and Qutb, as well as the movements they inspired, were indirectly responding to and arguing against in their work. Neither makes much of it, but throughout most of Mawdudi's life and all of Qutb's the most influential Muslim state in the world was making secular, tolerant civil government work and turning a welcoming face to the rest of the world. The center of the Muslim civic vision that radical Islam struggles to ignore was—and to a great degree still is—Turkey.

Mustafa Kemal Ataturk was born in 1881 in Salonica, today a city in Greece, but at the time a rich cultural possession of the Ottoman Empire. He was born Mustafa Kemal. Ataturk, a name of honor, he took after becoming the absolute ruler of the nation of Turkey. Fittingly, the most important figure in the shaping of modern, centrist Islam had been both a defender of the Ottoman cause and an agent of its demise. He was a graduate of Ottoman military schools and an officer in the Ottoman army, but in 1908 he took part in a revolutionary movement against the Ottoman sultan. At the close of the world war, Ataturk swept through what is now western Turkey and emerged as the most powerful warlord of a largely lawless period.

The era of Muslim empire lasted until the end of the First World War, when the final efforts of the Ottoman rulers of a third of Europe—even at the outset of the war, only a fragment of what their empire had been two centuries earlier—failed. In July 1923 a new national government under Ataturk's leadership signed the Lausanne Treaty with England, France, Greece, Italy, and the United States, setting, finally, the territory that would define the smaller, weaker Turkish nation in the world that emerged from the First World War. In October of that year, Ataturk declared that the new state was to be known as the Republic of Turkey. He quickly began a series of cultural transformations. What had been a nation led by local despots and clan leaders, who themselves had been led by a corrupt sultan reduced in rank to a caliph by the foreign powers who triumphed in the world war, became a modern Muslim state presided over by a secular leader. Ataturk sought at least some degree of representative government, rights for women, engagement with the wider world, and a judicial process based on civil law rather than the idiosyncratic interpretations of the Quran and the Hadith, the collected sayings and actions attributed to Muhammad.

Clearly Ataturk did not reach all these goals in his fifteen years as head of the new Turkish republic. Despotic Turkey would not be confused with the democratic nations of the West—England, France, or the United States—in the twenties or thirties, but the strides toward Ataturk's ideals were stunning, and the progress endured.

The relation of Islam to Turkey under Ataturk began to resemble the relation of classical Greek and Roman religious ideas to modern Athens and Rome, or the relation between modern Christianity and modern Western states today. Fundamentalists accused Ataturk of robbing Turkey of its religious core. Supporters of Ataturk's legacy pointed to Thomas Jefferson and declared that a separation of church and state protected both, reserving for religion the province of the soul, and for the state the province of material gain and worldly goods.

Ataturk pushed aside not only the imam's role in civic affairs but also the central symbols of Islam. He forbade religious dress in public, and even today public speech about a wide range of religious ideas can land a citizen of Turkey in jail. Simply put, Ataturk wanted less religion—indeed, just about no religion—in the public life of his nation, and he used his power as head of state to make that so. Defenders of Ataturk argue that faith was not so much repressed as balanced by a secular civic life for Turkey. Faith in the teaching of Islam now sat beside a civic faith. "The nation has placed its faith in the precept that all laws should be inspired by actual needs here on Earth as a basic fact of national life," Ataturk famously said, challenging his religious opponents directly. He declared in concert with the philosophers of the European Enlightenment that a religion can inspire the ideals of government but cannot provide the means of law, because while the good of the soul is not the business of government, the common good—the greatest good for the greatest number, measured in material things—is not the business of religion. Unto Caesar we render the body politic, and unto the Lord, unto Allah, we render the soul.

Ataturk never openly took a public stance to suppress religion, though his edicts had a dramatic effect in limiting religious practice and veiling Islam in the public sphere. Instead he portrayed himself as essentially a modern interpreter of Islam. "Our religion," he wrote, "does not advise our nation to be worthless, indolent, and inferior. To the contrary, God and also the Prophet order nations to protect their values and their honor." "If our religion was not compatible with logic and wisdom," he wrote, meaning by "logic and wisdom" modern science and openness to the modern world, "it would not be perfect and the last religion." Ataturk here invoked the core teaching of Islam: that it was indeed the last and perfect religion.

Directly to the question of the center and the fringe of Islamic thinking in his time, Ataturk wrote, "As you know, degenerates who have taken us in the wrong direction were mostly masked with a religious veil and have continuously deceived our pure and clear people with interpretations of religious rules. Read our history and listen. . . . You will see that all the evil which ruined, captivated, and destroyed our people always came from the infidels masked by religion."

Ataturk chose an enforced secularism as the path into the future for his nation. But his was not the only view of the future. No group strikes a greater contrast with Ataturk in its vision of Islamic society and governance than the Taliban, who ruled Afghanistan until the American rout following the bombing of the World Trade Center in September 2001. Although seventy years separate them, the dialogue between Ataturk and the rulers of the Afghan Taliban is an important one. What is the function of the state? Ataturk says it is to feed, clothe, and protect the people within the state, including women and children, and to provide them the greatest possible material and social benefits of living in the world as it is. Spiritual life is not the business of the state, but the social and material stability of a society properly governed provides room for personal, private spiritual and religious practice. The Taliban say the function of the state is to enforce the social codes of the Quran, and to empower local village and clan leaders to interpret and enforce those restrictions without restraint, following the example of the larger state. The souls of men, women, and children are to be protected by the state, even if that protection requires beating, starving, or killing them.

Today Pervez Musharraf, the president of Pakistan, faces a dilemma. His nation has been home to many of the most extreme Muslim fundamentalists, currently hosts hundreds of religious schools funded by groups dedicated to the most violent interpretations of Islam, and not long ago saw the killing of the American journalist Daniel Pearl, who was asked by his killer, "Are you a Jew?" moments before his throat was cut. Musharraf must balance the desire of much of his nation's citizenry to participate in the modern world, against a large and potent minority that supports the remnants of the Taliban and demands immediate and absolute fundamentalist rule. On his office wall hangs a portrait of Ataturk, a sign of hope for President Musharraf's Western supporters, among others.

To consider Just War philosophy in the Muslim tradition, then, we need to ask, in which Muslim tradition? The Muslim tradition of Saladin and Ataturk, similar to the Christian tradition of Jefferson or the Jewish tradition of Ben-Gurion? Or the Muslim tradition of the Taliban, similar to the Christian tradition of the Crusades or the Jewish tradition of, say, Meier Kahane and Nathan Lewin?

## IS THE MESSAGE OF ISLAM TO DESTROY?

To understand the most pressing questions about war today, we must have some sensible response to the notion that Islam is a singularly violent religion, a conspiracy against Jews and Christians. The only reasonable conclusion we can draw about Islam in light of the Jewish, Christian, and Muslim states that have risen and fallen in the past two thousand years is that Islam is just as brutal, just as ugly, just as beneficent, and just as beautiful in its teachings about war and peace as the other faiths are. The darkest aspects of the Quran are no worse than the darkest aspects of the Hebrew Bible; the acts of terror planned and perpetrated against non-Muslim infidels in our lifetimes still pale against the crimes committed against civilian Muslim populations by the Christian Crusaders of the eleventh and twelfth centuries, by the British Empire a hundred years ago, and by the Orthodox Christians of Serbia not ten years ago.

The lessons of Islam and Judaism and Christianity about Just War thinking lie less in the specifics of what each religion explicitly teaches and more in the larger structure of dialogue and debate all three faiths help support. All three faiths reveal that Just War philosophy must ask the individual to judge, not simply to obey. Fundamentalism proposes that there is a path to heaven, though a narrow one, available to all who hew closely to it. But a useful Just War theory cannot glibly accept the idea that the warrior may go to heaven. By definition, the warrior is stained by blood. Any decent Just War philosophy cannot begin by closing its eyes to that blood and dreaming instead of the afterlife, whether it is the Muslim paradise of black-eyed virgins or the cloudless climes of Christian tradition.

The central question of Just War philosophy is not, How can I get to heaven? It is not, How can I be good? (Any serious moral consideration of war soon enough faces the obvious fact that the individual who plans or makes war is already lost from the quality of innocence that every religion reveres.) Instead it is a question of some subtlety: In which direction does my duty lie? The framing of the question itself confesses a degree of moral failure—not to have done better, not to have taken another road when roads diverged—and a sense of being already lost at the point of deciding whether or not to fight.

# 5

# THE QUESTIONS OF

# SEQUENCE AND SCALE

❦

ONE OF THE GREAT TRAGEDIES in thinking about war is the habit of forgetting about Just War ideas in times of peace. The essence of Just War philosophy is that sometimes a terrible sequence of events has unfolded to the point that war is the least worst option. But if we accept this notion in times of crisis, we must also bear it in mind in times without crisis, when a moral perspective might prevent the war that follows from our poor decisions. The image comes to mind of President Carter toasting the shah of Iran and declaring his government a good and decent friend of the United States while thousands of Iranians were being held by Iran's CIA-trained secret police, the Savak, regularly tortured and facing the prospect of execution at the whim of their jailors. Not long after, the uprising against the shah erupted, and the first modern Muslim theocracy was born. When 52 American hostages were taken by Iranian religious students with the support of their government and ultimately held captive for 444 days, there was overwhelming popular support in the United States for war against Iran. President Carter resisted, striking the pose of a patient man of peace. It is hard to reconcile that pose with the image of the tuxedo-clad Carter toasting the shah not a year earlier. Facing the decision of war in response to the hostage situation, Just War thinking might have lead us to believe that, yes, after all other options had failed, some degree of military action would be ugly but the best possible solution. But Just War thinking is badly abused if it is brought to bear only when the hand is upon the sword. The moral aspects of other decisions, such as supporting and training the Iranian secret police, must also be part of the equation. We must ask questions of similar moral substance as our nation involves itself in the affairs of so many others around the world, and we must hold a similarly high standard for what is right.

The rivers of money and tons of weapons that the United States gave to Saddam Hussein and Osama bin Laden when Washington thought of them as friends, or at least as the enemies of our enemies, are particularly vivid examples. Either both were once good and have now become evil, as President Bush has called them, or our nation's moral sensibility was otherwise engaged when we decided to arm and train the forces of Saddam and bin Laden. And there are no shortages of similar examples today, from Syria to Colombia. If we wheel out the moral apparatus of Just War thinking only when it has come time to kill, we are guilty—just as the most cynical churchmen in thrall to governing parties have been guilty—of looking toward higher truths only to excuse ourselves for the evil we do.

The question here, of when we choose to exercise moral thinking in national policy, is a large one. It is part of the even larger questions of sequence and scale, of figuring out when the starting point of any issue we wish to see from a moral perspective really occurs. In our age, the scale of things can telescope or collapse in the blink of an eye, as a man wakes in the morning in Washington, D.C., and prepares for bed that night in Kabul, or as the anger of a man in the Middle East sends a missile into the heart of Europe. Ours is an age in which we can watch war by television and see moments of destruction and salvation open and close—lives shaken, taken, and left not quite as we found them—before we rise from our chairs or manage even to close our eyes. The question of where events begin is a profound one, and one that makes all the difference between right and wrong.

Consider, for example, the issue of self-defense. The three major religious Just War traditions recognize self-defense as a fundamental starting point of Just War. Jewish doctrine has a separate category of wars of defense; Catholic theology today points to the wars of defense as being in the most complete accordance with the several criteria for a Just War; and Islam specifically speaks of defensive Jihad as the only legitimate kind of war in an age without a caliph. But what do we mean by defense? Is suicide bombing, even attacking the World Trade Center, possibly defensive? Al Qaeda talks of the need to defend the holy ground of Mecca and the rest of Saudi Arabia from invading, crusading American troops, heavy on the ground there since the end of the Gulf War. In Al Qaeda's vocabulary, they are defending Islam by striking out against the men and women at work in the twin towers. But can that understanding of self-defense be legitimate?

As a way into these compelling and complex questions, consider the question of when the first Gulf War began. One easy answer is that it began on the day that Saddam Hussein's Iraqi army invaded Kuwait. Another is that it began the day the first

U.S. bombs fell on Baghdad. But what of the experience of the American soldier called to duty in the Gulf? When did that soldier's war begin? Where are the moral decision points? Or consider the task of the military planner, or even the president of the United States. President George H. W. Bush said he saw Saddam's invasion of Kuwait as the opening act in the war. But it was the massing of Iraqi troops on the Saudi Arabian border that some historians believe led Bush to contemplate war, because Saudi Arabia was a more important U.S. ally and trading partner than tiny Kuwait. Still greater historical perspective can bring us back at least to the creation of the modern state of Iraq, an event set in motion when the Young Turks in 1908 took control of the Ottoman Empire, which by then had swallowed the traditional lands of Iraq and Mesopotamia.

In 1917, as part of their final sweep to victory in the First World War, British troops occupied Baghdad, and the seeds of a general anti-European and anti-Western outlook were sown. Britain's initial posture toward Arab peoples was one of liberation: they declared that the centuries of Ottoman Empire were ended and that Arab nations could now rise as independent states. But in 1920 the League of Nations created the British Mandate in the area that is now Iraq, Jordan, and Israel, and Britain ran the area like a colony. In 1938, Iraqi King Ghazi massed his troops on the border of Kuwait, preparing to invade, but died in an auto accident before the campaign could begin; in the transition to a successor government, the invasion was put off.

Through the early years of the Second World War, Iraq was ruled by local monarchs with varying degrees of pan-Arab feelings and friendliness toward Britain. In 1941, though, a coup installed an anti-British government with open ties to Nazi

Germany. In response, Britain invaded and occupied the country. Pro-British forces ruled until 1958, when a military coup brought Abdul-Karim Qassem to power. In 1961, Britain declared the independence of Kuwait, ending its nominal rule over that nation, and Qassem immediately declared it to be part of Iraq, threatening to invade. Britain sent a detachment of troops to Kuwait to signal its opposition, and Qassem chose instead to recognize the borders of an independent Kuwait. Two years later Qassem was assassinated, and the rule of the Ba'ath socialists began. In 1979, Saddam Hussein took power, nominally to restore integrity to the Ba'athists, but in fact to begin his own imperial reign.

This history matters for several reasons. From the highest perspective, it shows that the beginnings of war come at different times for different people. A Ba'athist might see the Gulf War as part of a struggle that began with the corruption of the Ba'ath ideal sometime in the mid-1960s: what we call the Gulf War he will call a battle in the larger struggle for Arab socialism and self-determination. A pan-Arab nationalist might propose that the war began with Britain's failure to allow self-determination following the First World War. And extremist Muslim perspective might go back centuries to the Ottoman domination of Iraq's tribal areas and propose the Gulf War as part of a millennium of foreign domination of Muslims by non-Muslims in the West and errant Muslims from the Turkish north. A non-Muslim villager invested in local clan tradition might view the Gulf War as part of the eternal conflict between the clan and outsiders, whether the outsiders be Muslim invaders, national Ba'athist troops, or American soldiers.

To watch the Gulf War unfold from a living room in the United States, as I did, is to be blind and deaf to these other perspectives. Even the most attentive Americans had heard little about Iraq in the years before the Gulf War, save cursory media coverage of the long-running and brutal Iran-Iraq War. The Iraqi invasion of Kuwait prompted only minor media coverage. The news media were not sure that, as they say, there was a real story there until hints emerged from the White House that this particular bit of faraway geopolitics might matter a great deal. Only after Iraqi troops were spotted by U.S. intelligence satellites massing on the Saudi border, and the White House spoke out firmly, did U.S. media see a story emerging.

How important are these differences in perspective? How much should it matter to Americans that a tribal villager on the Tigris River sees a war differently than we do? A great deal, it turns out. The attack on the World Trade Center on September 11, 2001, makes that vividly clear.

I witnessed that attack as many Americans did. I had heard a rumor that a small plane had struck one of the towers before I left my home in suburban Chicago that morning. I drove into work with the famous image in my mind of a 1940s pilot standing in a destroyed office in the Empire State Building, beside the shattered plane he had driven into its side. But the radio cut away from the usual morning news to tell the story of the second attack on the Trade Center, the intense fire and smoke, and eventually the bodies falling from upper floors. By the time I passed the Sears Tower in downtown Chicago, not far from my office, I could see the driver of every car nearby craning to look fearfully toward the tower's upper floors.

As a native New Yorker, my first reactions were emotional and personal. As I began to think about the broader issues, and in particular about the motives of the attackers, I made many mistakes in perspective. Once it became clear that the attackers were Arab terrorists, I assumed they were poor and uneducated. I fixed on the images of the Palestinian refugee camps in Jordan, Lebanon, and the Occupied Territories of the West Bank and Gaza. I had some understanding of the deprivations endured by people in those camps, and I knew those deprivations formed part of the basis for the angry Arab politics of the Middle East. But I also knew that however much responsibility for that deprivation belonged to Israel, the Arab governments themselves were quite harsh in their treatment of Palestinians generally and the residents of refugee camps in particular. Why, I asked, would an angry young man in a camp in Jordan, denied citizenship rights and freedom of movement by the Jordanian government, turn his anger toward Washington rather than toward Amman? I knew that Palestinian refugees had waged war against their Arab hosts in Jordan and Lebanon not many years earlier, but now their anger had been deflected from the Arab states and focused on Israel and indirectly on the United States.

I took for granted that poverty was their principal motivator, and that if they were given the freedoms of an immigrant in an open nation, they would eventually prosper and put their hatreds aside to build homes and lives for their families. The main culprits, I believed, were the governments of the nations in which they lived. That those nations had redirected Palestinian anger toward the United States seemed a kind of terrible political brilliance.

But then, like many Americans, I learned more. It turned out that the World Trade Center attackers were relatively prosperous and well educated. And the anti-American anger they represented was more intense than I had imagined. More to the point, it was not an anger that spared the local Arab regimes. The literature of the extreme Muslim movements that share a murderous hatred of the United States is in fact infused with a sense of history that I had not imagined in my casual theories of why young Muslims were angry. Their philosophy joined the United States with the local regimes, and with Israel, as distinct manifestations of the same evil. Beginning with the Ottoman Empire, native Arab culture had been dominated by outsiders after close to a thousand years of remarkable civic accomplishment, military power, and commercial influence. The outsider Turks were replaced by the outsider British, in this vision a movement from bad to worse. Then the outsider British were joined in 1948 by the outsider Jews, a quantum leap in the perception of violation by outsiders. U.S. influence grew as Israel became its proxy state and American commercial culture began to filter into many aspects of daily Arab life, from T-shirts and sneakers to television and fast food. The evil local rulers were seen from the radical Muslim perspective as proxies of the evil British, who installed them, and the evil Americans, who filled their pockets with money and drained their sands of oil. The logic of this worldview is clean and easy to communicate. And it appeals as much to the middle class, with its awareness of the world's view of Arab peoples and its potential to play a role in governments that might replace existing regimes, as it does to the poor.

Many Americans see September 11 as an unprovoked attack and the beginning of a war. Certainly from the perspective of any man, woman, or child lost on September 11, there was no provocation and no moral connection to the lives of people across the globe who see New York City as a symbol somehow connected to the Jordanian or Israeli soldier who humiliates them. But the alternative perspective is also true to a degree. Just as the Trade Center widow did not chose to participate in, and was perhaps not aware of, the large-scale politics of empire that connected the United States to the lives of the Trade Center attackers, so the child killed by a rocket fired by an American-built helicopter into her family's home in the West Bank was unaware of the larger politics that her life would in its final moments become part of. Or, to take a perhaps more appropriate example, the teenage Saudi or Pakistani student shipped off to a radical Muslim school that teaches him to hate Israelis and Americans and prepares him to die fighting them has not necessarily chosen to live that life but in all likelihood has found himself thrust into it.

This is the existential moment of war: we do not begin at the beginning. We begin in the middle. As soldier, as head of state, as citizen, we become aware at some point that we are facing dire decisions. Whatever causes we can name for the horrors we can see unfolding will be inadequate to the task of making moral sense of the choices that face us. They will be stories we tell ourselves about why we contemplate doing the awful business of war, but they will be inadequate and incomplete.

Knowing this, what are we to do? Is the soldier about to go kill and perhaps die in Iraq to say *no*, because this is a war about oil, or a war about the British Mandate of 1920, or a war about the last days of the First World War—and none of that is worth fighting for? All of these causes are true, to a degree. But the war in Iraq is also a war against a head of state who has killed large numbers of his own citizens, who is at best a fascist and at worst a genocidal maniac set on enlarging his empire and prepared to vaporize the civilian populations of nations he sees as enemies. How do we balance the bad motives with the good? How much stain does the soldier or the statesman bear for the base motives and the bad acts that come bound together with the noble motives and good ends that represent the goals of a given war?

The only answer to these questions lies in the principle that Just Wars are wars about the future and not about the past. In the end, if one looks closely enough at the history of any nation or military force, one will find a stained past. To the same degree that the argument against slavery in the American South is not weakened—indeed, not even addressed—by the observation that African leaders were part of the slave trade, that they themselves kept slaves in some quarters of their continent, so the history of empire does not bear on any nation's acts of war *if those acts are acts of self-defense or acts of aid to innocent third parties*. To the extent that Just War thinking demands of a nation that its motives for war must be to end harm and build a better future, legitimate questions of context and history should not outweigh the moral imperative to do good.

These questions must be raised and answered. The burden of leadership is to share the process of addressing them—for the French to say yes, our colonial domination of the Ivory Coast was wrong, but still we will aid innocent people there who call for our help; for the British and the Turks to say yes, our colonial domination of Central Asia and the Middle East was wrong, but we shall still aid the innocents there who call for our help; for Americans to say yes, we have done wrong in many corners of the globe, but we shall not fail to do good today because of that. The greater imperative is to apply the lessons of the past to current conduct apart from decisions about war. Are we making mistakes today similar to those we made decades or centuries before? Is someone else's story, a story that might end in war, beginning somewhere today—in Colombia, in Yemen, in other places we know little about where American soldiers ply their trade?

The ultimate lesson of questions of sequence and scale is to supply more questions, to make it harder to ignore the small effects we have in far places that tomorrow may become crises, and to demand that we draw moral connections between the wars that may be just today and the small acts that may lead to wars tomorrow, wars we can prevent.

# 6

## SAYING NO AND
## SAYING YES:
## PROTEST AND THE
## INTEGRITY OF LANGUAGE
## IN TIMES OF WAR

WAR BY ITS NATURE suspends the limits of human decency: remove the imperative of Thou shall not kill and you set in motion events that may become most horrible. Because larger moral principles are suspended, a constant attention to small acts becomes more important.

In the United States we have seen a "professionalization" of the armed forces. Career soldiers are further removed from the values and experience of the broader culture than an army of conscripts would be. Career soldiers tend to fight better, are less troubled by moral scruples in their work, and are not as likely to be shocked by war's ugly nature as are men and women taken roughly at random from the civilian population. Because of this, a long-term professional army increases the importance of dissent, the importance of balancing war's necessity with its essential horror.

The question of dissent is raised by the very act of thinking Just War thoughts. At its best, Just War thinking operates by helping leaders, citizens, and soldiers exercise restraint and forgo the wars that will do more harm than good. But in practical terms, the mechanism of the state is such that its collective intelligence and moral conscience are continually being reinvented. They are not fixed qualities that can be exercised on simple terms; rather, they are the product of open and often loud give and take. Protest is thus at the very heart of a state's ability to act, and influences its orientation when acting. The government that is swayed by its citizens' beliefs is a better one than it would otherwise be. And for all the elected representatives, councils, polls, and polemics, the citizenry often must speak to its leaders in the open streets. Protest does not necessarily deliver answers to the powers that be, but it is a powerful tool for making sure that questions are posed—the very essence of Just War thinking.

These lessons apply especially to the United States of America, a nation born of protest and revolt. The tradition of popular sovereignty—of the will of the people trumping all other sources of authority and legitimacy—runs deeper here than in any other nation. But the burden of citizenship is not so simple. The basic act of protest—saying no to a policy or program—is far easier than saying yes to a better alternative. Protest is a responsibility of every citizen when government actions violate the will of the citizenry. Every voice is capable of saying no, and is perhaps even obligated to say no in some cases. But saying yes to an alternative is harder. Just War thinking is, in part, the work of saying no. But that is the easy part. Just War thinking is also the work of saying yes, and that work is infinitely harder.

Protest against war generally consists of one of two distinct messages. One is the message that *this* war is wrong—a mistake of policy. The other is that *all* war is wrong by its nature. The first message, which seems on its surface less extreme, is actually the harder of the two for a nation mobilized for war to endure. It takes an everything or nothing position, and if the statesman and soldier are not entirely convinced of its merits, it does little good. The second is a different story. It sparks the humanity of everyone who hears its message. War *is* wrong. Particularly when war is necessary, it is too easy to be distracted from the moral fact, and the protester serves a vital social function for every party to war, from the White House to the field of battle, in keeping that moral clarity at hand and calling our nation's soldiers back from believing too deeply in the missions we have given them—to kill, and perhaps to die.

John Updike has written that "to say that war is madness is like saying that sex is madness: true enough, from the standpoint of a stateless eunuch, but merely a provocative epigram for those who must make their arrangements in the world as a given." To be a citizen, he implies, is to participate in the collective appetite and passions of a community that will inevitably make war. But the most noble protester will continue to say "war is madness" if only to urge reflection on the warrior and the policymaker—if only to keep the soldier and statesman from loving war too much.

The protester reminds us of the obvious, so that our compromises with reality do not themselves become the foundation for a reality far worse. Thus Just War thinking can become a tool for caution and resistance to war. As Professor Lisa Sowle Cahill of Boston College has written, "Christian leaders should be using just-war criteria to raise questions about military actions, to mount criticism, to urge caution. . . . There are plenty of other people out there who are willing to say that the war is justified and that it must go forward. That's not the role that we have to fill." For this professor, protest is not an all-or-nothing game. Unlike Augustine's notion of every war having only one just side, Cahill's notion of protest allows legitimate roles for both the soldier who fights and the protester who militates against his fighting. Writing in October 2001, reflecting on the terrorist attacks in New York that September, Cahill struck a personal note: "Although I really can't stand patriotic hymns in church . . . —they're almost blasphemous—I did notice, as *America the Beautiful* was being sung against my will at Mass in recent weeks, that it said 'God mend thy every flaw, confirm thy soul in self-control, thy liberty in law.' It really seemed the kind of prayer that Christians should say for their country." The message was very much the message of the loyal opposition: be better, America; live up to your ideals. Be soulful, embrace liberty, especially in time of war. This is good protest, a fine example of loyal opposition, in this case perhaps more loyal than opposed.

## AN ISRAELI SOLDIER WALKING TO THE SHOWER

Protest lives in the space between action and reflection. To take up arms against a regime is not to protest that regime so much as to make war against it. Protest ends where revolt begins. At the other extreme, pure thought is not protest, and private conversation, not matter how intense, is not protest either. Protest requires an audience.

The Israeli writer Ari Shavit, a newspaper columnist, had exactly that as he reported for his annual reserve army duty in 1991, though he did not expect to call upon that audience for his own form of protest against his government's policies in the Occupied Territories. Shavit wound up writing an essay published first in Hebrew in Israel and then in English in the *New York Review of Books*, under the title "On Gaza Beach." His essay offers two compelling images of protest, one that edges from reflection into protest, and another that pushes beyond protest into rank destruction.

Like all men of a certain age, Shavit is called upon each year for a few weeks of active military duty in the Israeli Defense Forces. In 1991, he tells his readers, "instead of taking part in military exercises, I am a guard." Shavit takes up his post guarding Palestinian prisoners at the Gaza Beach Internment Facility, a place that reminds him and his fellow reservists, in its grim feeling and function, of Nazi concentration camps. He understands the differences, of course. "And yet," Shavit writes, "the unjust analogy with those other camps of fifty years ago won't go away. It is not suggested by anti-Israel propaganda. It is in the language the soldiers use as a matter of course: when A gets up to do guard duty in the interrogation section, he says, 'I'm off, late for the Inquisition.'

". . . And N, who has strong right-wing views, grumbles for anyone who will listen that the place resembles a concentration camp.

"M, with a thin smile, explains that he has accumulated so many days in reserve duty during the intifada that soon they will promote him to a senior Gestapo official."

Once the context is clear, much of Shavit's piece takes the form of an interior monologue. "At the end of the watch," he writes, "on your way from the tent to the shower you sometimes hear horrible screams as you walk in your shorts and clogs, a towel slung over your shoulder, toilet kit in hand, and from the other side of the galvanized tin fence of the interrogation section come hair-raising human screams. Literally hair raising." This image of Shavit the naked soldier, the man stripped down to an ununiformed humanity as he hears those screams, is important. His is the unguarded human response of the citizen soldier, not the hardened intensity of the career warrior. "Try not to be oversensitive, you say to yourself. Don't get carried away, don't jump to conclusions. Doesn't every nation have its basements, its special services, its 'security' problem? It just happens to be your bad luck to have been sent to a place where you can hear exactly how the thing sounds." Not duty, not a chosen profession, but bad luck.

Shavit's ultimate response to his experience is the article he writes. He does not march on a government office, paint placards, or avoid serving. He simply writes, connecting his military experience with his civilian life and bringing his story to a broad audience. His article ends this way: The Palestinians "have deprived us, in the most unambiguous way, of the possibility of an 'enlightened occupation.' They have forced us to choose: territories or decency. Occupation or fairness. And, yes, that is indeed the question of the hour. An acute and urgent question, demanding an answer at once. It is not, at this hour, a matter of territories in exchange for peace. It is a matter of territories in exchange for our humanity."

The framing of this question for a large audience is Shavit's act of protest, one that had a substantial impact throughout his

143

home country and to a degree in ours. In the middle of his article, Shavit wrote that "in the forty months of intifada, more than ten thousand Israeli citizens in uniform have walked between the fences, have heard the screams, have seen the young being led in and out—and the country has been quiet, has flourished.

"And Prime Minister Shamir has continued to believe that everything's all right, more or less." In fact, Shamir was voted out of office not long after Shavit's article appeared. Yitzhak Rabin took his place and quietly entered into talks with the Palestinian Liberation Organization and others that created real hope for lasting change, including the prospect of an Israeli-sanctioned Palestinian state. The image of Rabin on the White House lawn reluctantly taking the hand of Yassir Arafat within the embrace of President Clinton is a lasting reminder of the degree to which Rabin moved off the complacent position Shamir held in Shavit's portrait of the earlier prime minister. That image of Rabin, Clinton, and Arafat is also something of a memorial for Rabin, who was killed not long after as he spoke in a public square in Israel. Rabin's killer was a young Israeli, a Jewish student who, like many in his fundamentalist enclave, believed that Rabin was bargaining away lands over which God had granted Jews, and only Jews, dominion. He believed that Rabin was showing weakness in the face of the Canaanites and Amalekites, and so he took it upon himself to destroy Rabin. This act was beyond protest; it was political violence of the ugliest sort, the product of fringe fundamentalism, a force on both sides of the Israeli/Palestinian conflict from which an enormous flood of additional violence and suffering has since flowed.

As Lisa Cahill noted, protest in the Just War tradition is not about taking up arms, nor is protest necessarily about taking sides. In its most effective forms, protest does not so much say Stop! as it says Think! Thus the power—personal and political—of an act of protest like Shavit's. Thus the power, too, of the Lafayette Park drummers.

## THE DRUMMERS OF LAFAYETTE PARK

Lafayette Park sits across from the White House. During the first Gulf War a group of protesters in that park found their purpose. They had been holding regular protests against any number of the sins of capitalism, with particular emphasis on issues important to American Indians. They beat a number of drums as part of their protest, generally keeping within the legal limit of 60 decibels. At noon, among the traffic and other city noises of the capital, 60 decibels is not terribly loud. At night it is a good deal louder, and in the early hours of the morning loud enough to keep a resident of Pennsylvania Avenue awake. Federal park police took a number of steps to make the protesters uncomfortable and to shut them out of the park whenever they exceeded 60 decibels, yet the protests continued around the clock during all of the 1991 war in Iraq, during which American forces took the lead in a victory that no doubt saved many lives but also took by many estimates more than 100,000 Iraqi lives in the process.

I was an ambivalent supporter of the Gulf War. I was more anti-Saddam than pro-American invasion, but I took the overall effort to be a tragic necessity, and historical perspective has only strengthened this position. Yet I loved those protesters. At one public occasion during the war, President Bush made the terrible mistake of whispering within camera range that those drums were driving him crazy. The protesters of course were thrilled, and their energy to keep the drums sounding around the clock was renewed by this unplanned hint of their effectiveness. Even though I supported that war, I was glad the drums were there. It seemed right that a national leader should not sleep well as he prosecuted a war that killed people by the tens of thousands.

The beginning of Just War theory, as we have seen, comes with the beginning of the state. Thucydides raises the first questions, and Cicero, not all that long before the year 1, offers the first answers. Augustine offers the first moral statement that transcends the state, and Kant, Hegel, and Clausewitz see the modern state in motion and raise the most important questions about how war works and whose interests it serves in the modern world we recognize around us today. Each of these thinkers proposes answers to the fundamental questions of Just War, and each answer builds upon those that have come earlier. Yet none offers the *answer*, not even Augustine and Aquinas, who propose to deliver a moral system that should function without exception or hesitation. The entire Just War platform stands on the shaky pillars of phrases like "right intention" and "just cause," and leaves us perilously close to the idea that in order for a war to be good, its component pieces must be good—and for the pieces to be good, the larger purpose of the war must be good. And so we wind up saying little beyond the obvious—that only Just Wars are just.

As individuals, until we make clear moral judgments about what is most precious and what is most evil, we cannot act morally in matters of war. If one is content to stop at that point and thus say no to all wars, he or she will find much friendly company. But that abdicates the most important questions of the age. It hides from the darkest aspect of being human and allows others to sin on one's behalf. From any perspective of leadership, it is simply not adequate. Recall that Augustine felt that the best justified war is not the war of self-defense but the war to aid innocent third parties being attacked by others. This is the duty to act that Just War thinking, at its best, enables. Protest helps us clarify our purpose and helps us maintain a sense of proportion in what we do. Protest reminds us of the vital necessity of national conscience even—especially—as we exercise our collective power to kill. Without protest, and without the witness of ordinary Americans to our nation's acts of war, we may find ourselves the owners of victories that serve short-term ends but change the character of our nation beyond our collective intent. If excellence in battle is not balanced by ordinary conscience, we may find our warriors serving us all too well.

Consider, for example, this concluding scene from Bob Woodward's book about the American war in Afghanistan, *Bush at War*. On February 5, 2002, a group of American soldiers and intelligence operatives gathered at a site near the town of Gardez. One buried a small fragment of the remains of the World Trade Center under the spot they surrounded. "One of the men said a prayer," Woodward writes. "Then he said, 'We consecrate this spot as an everlasting memorial to the brave Americans who died on September 11, so that all who would seek to do her harm will know that America will not stand by and watch terror prevail.

" 'We will export death and violence to the four corners of the earth in defense of our great nation.' "

Wrong as it would be to criticize or condemn these men for their extraordinary ability to do so well precisely what they have been trained to do, particularly in the immediate aftermath of September 11, this scene ought to trouble any American who hears of it. These are the rough men ready to make war about whom Orwell wrote, and indeed they sacrifice much for the sake of the rest of us. Yet their business is the most awful business that men and women engage in. Their determination is admirable, but the seeming ease with which they wear the cloak of executioner, in the very name of America and Americans, is stunning. Just as these soldiers feel compelled to unite the scene of their battles with the scene of the terrorist assault on New York City that set those battles in motion, so the observer feels a profound need to unite the brutal intentions and effects of their work with a clear voice of protest, a voice that says Think!, that says This is awful, that asks in every instance, Can we do better? Can we be more decent?

A vital part of doing better and thinking clearly is using language with integrity—to call a war a war (not a police action or a program of regime change), a defeat a defeat (not a strategic withdrawal or a rearward advance), and the innocent victims of war exactly that (not collateral damage or enemy civilians).

## JUST WAR AND THE INTEGRITY OF LANGUAGE

Writing from London late in 1945, just as England was reforming its national sense of itself after the Second World War, George Orwell published an essay called "Politics and the English Language." Among the most frequently anthologized and reprinted pieces, it is very much about the language of war. In it Orwell writes, "In our time, political speech and writing are largely the defense of the indefensible. Things like the continuance of British rule in India, the Russian purges and deportations, the dropping of the atom bombs on Japan, can indeed be defended, but only by arguments which are too brutal for most people to face, and which do not square with the professed aims of political parties. Thus political language has come to consist largely of euphemism, question-begging, and sheer cloudy vagueness."

Orwell's observations are especially important to the task of Just War thinking. Just War philosophy is, after all, built of words, and only when those words are clear and direct will the tools of moral thought about war be truly useful. Just War thinking intentionally imposes a struggle with the meaning of a word like "legitimate"—in the phrase "legitimate authority"—for those who wish to think in earnest about these things. And certainly we need a clear common understanding of a word like "soldier" if we are to think and talk about war with any moral sense. Yet the reasonable limits of interpretation are routinely exceeded by governments intent on preserving surface appearances that just are not so. They are also routinely exceeded by protesters and revolutionaries intent on creating as stark a contrast as they can between their own vision and that of the status quo—a contrast often served by calling something black or white that is in fact grey.

As a case in point, consider the November 2002 remarks of President George W. Bush in Prague. With the prospect of a second war against Iraq looming, Bush went to the Czech Republic to join with other leaders of NATO nations in recognizing a number of former Soviet client states as new members of the alliance. In his remarks, he said, "Members recently added to NATO and those invited to join bring greater clarity to purposes of our Alliance, because they understand the lessons of the last century. Those with fresh memories of tyranny know the value of freedom. Those who have lived through a struggle of good against evil are never neutral between them." All hard to argue against, but as an expression of respect for the experience of ordinary citizens of Eastern Europe during the decades of Soviet domination, this language seems willfully ignorant of the many moral contradictions and the large grey areas in that experience.

To listen to average people from the Czech Republic, Poland, or East Germany talk about their lives behind the Iron Curtain is to hear of fears that friends and family—loved ones—were spies for the government. All citizens of Soviet client states faced the prospect of bartering petty betrayals for a better job, a better apartment, or perhaps simply for relief from the relentless suspiciousness of the powers that be. A parent might provide scraps of information about a friend, neighbor, or even a spouse in exchange for a job or a university seat for a child. An employee might report on an employer, a student on a teacher, a servant on a high government functionary. This was a way of life that cut across every social distinction of education, occupation, and ambition. And it was almost universally taken for granted. Social trust was largely extinct, if only because the average citizen knew well enough his or her own betrayals. Is that the moral clarity of good against evil of which President Bush spoke?

An even more extreme case of the same rhetorical excess involves the two Koreas. A few months before his Prague speech, President Bush declared North Korea—along with Iran and Iraq—to be part of an Axis of Evil, in his memorable phrase, a phrase clearly drawn from the Second World War phrase book. South Koreans are profoundly aware of their differences with the North, and of the great deprivations that an obviously failed regime there has brought about. Yet their strongest feelings toward North Korea are feelings of brotherhood. They want positive change, but they would hardly characterize the North as evil. On the ground in Seoul—where I was traveling on business when George Bush made his Axis of Evil speech—I had the strong impression that the president was seeing a situation of the richest complexity—a situation in which two nations hosted divided families, divergent economies, radically different ways of living and thinking and seeing the world, but still shared a deep common heritage and a powerful filial bond—through the narrowest geopolitical lens. My hosts, in fact, were surprised when I told them that I would like to visit the demilitarized zone between the two Koreas during my free time. And when I arrived there, I understood why. The stream of people heading to the visitors center and then, after a long bus ride through American military outposts, to an observation post, fell into two categories: foreigners, mostly Americans and Japanese, and older Koreans, many of them veterans of the war that we call the Korean War, and many with relatives living in the North. Younger Koreans generally do not make the trip; it places the division of their larger nation too vividly in front of them, forcing them to confront a literal border that most prefer to see as an aberration, a mistake largely the product of warring foreign empires that will soon enough be corrected.

So why President Bush's language of "evil"? Why this most extreme simplification and condemnation? A too simple answer is, because that's the way this man thinks. But this does little beyond rephrasing the question—Why, then, does he think in such simple terms? Ultimately this kind of simplification, even if it is deeply held, becomes a form of propaganda, the act of representing the complexity of the world in simple terms for the sake of a political end. To talk so incessantly about good and evil, without the nuance of complex experience present at least in the margins, is to use the language of morality precisely to avoid the real substance of moral work. This is particularly true when we talk about war, which generally inhabits the grey area of moral thinking and requires a vocabulary that suits a situation of necessary sin and moral action that is at best least worst. Consider Orwell, again, on the language of war: "euphemism, question begging, and sheer cloudy vagueness." After September 11, George Bush said that the task facing the armies of America was to "protect all that is good." This is scarcely euphemistic, and President Bush deserves some praise for the clarity of his own belief and his lack of waffling. But at some point the simplicity of overeager moral judgment commits the same sins as "sheer cloudy vagueness." The process of moral judgment is cloistered within the White House, and the rest of us wind up with nothing to argue about. We are left simply to labor in the service of all that our leaders declare to be good.

Like the question of protest, the matter of clarity and nuance in language does not sit at the center of Just War thinking, but it sits at the vital place where thinking meets action. The language of leadership—and the language of the coffeehouse and the kitchen table—both communicates and shapes the principles that drive policy, and in some cases war. If Just War principles are understood and reflected upon, but communicated poorly, the exercise will do little good. If our leaders communicate only the conclusions they reach about the moral challenges we face as a nation, leaving out of view the process of judgment, the moral work of the citizenry is less to think than to hope. We are left with the hope that our leaders are wise and good—the kind of hope to which history is seldom kind.

## "WE ARE ALL SOLDIERS"

Beyond the words of politicians and power brokers, the intellectual and moral limits of language are also bent and broken by ordinary people driven by desperation, or by hope, to declare that things are comprehensible even when they are not. Thus horror is said to be normal, hate is said to be reason, and theft is said to be justice. And, at times, children are said to be soldiers.

Picture a group of French children, standing together in a field at summer camp. They salute the French flag and sing the French national anthem, *La Marseillaise*: "Tremble, tyrants and treacherous ones, the disgrace of all parties. Tremble! Your parricide at last will receive its reward. All are soldiers to fight you. If they fall, our young heroes, France will produce more anew, all ready to fight against you." What does it mean for these children to declare that "all are soldiers," presumably including these children themselves?

Of course children love to pretend to be soldiers, in a different way than they love to pretend to be bakers or bus drivers or professional wrestlers. To pretend to be a soldier is more like pretending to be a police officer or a fireman—not only to be an adult and to have a job but, more important, to serve the common good. The opportunity to play at making a sacrifice for the common good, and then go back to being children in time for milk and cookies, is deeply attractive.

But *La Marseillaise* does not take this kind of enlightened view of children's play. Yes, children may love to sing the anthem and imagine that through their words alone they are helping to shore up the defenses of France. But in fact they are not soldiers, and by saying so they make a statement about language as much as they do about soldiers. Moral thinking about war demands that we defend the border between literal identity and metaphor. Violence is violence; soldiers are soldiers. Words are not violence. Schoolchildren are not soldiers.

We can easily add to this list of the obvious the fact that people are not insects, though incitement to massive killing of Tutsi civilians by Hutus in Rwanda in 1994 included radio broadcasts urging Hutus to kill the Tutsi insects. This vision of racial difference among Rwandans was not limited to the uneducated: University of Southern California religion professor Donald Miller has described how "a well-educated Rwandan told me that his Hutu pastor refused to serve Communion to Tutsis prior to the genocide, because he did not think insects were worthy to eat and drink the body and blood of Christ."

People are not insects, and people are not vermin, even though the U.S. Marine Corps publication *Leatherneck* reported in May 1945 that what the Marines faced on the home islands of Japan was "a gigantic task of extermination." Nor are people monkeys, though in the 1944 film *The Fighting Seabees*, John Wayne memorably declared that his job was to kill the "bug-eyed monkeys of Tojo."

This question of the literal truth is a matter both of how we fight—soldiers cannot be just in their actions if they do not regard their opponents as human, even taking into account the bluster and psychology of destruction—and why we fight: the belief that others are not fully human and do not deserve what they have (at least as much as we do, when we feel we want it) is entirely outside the bounds of Just War. These examples support a vital principle of Just War for our time: a Just War acknowledges the humanity of all parties, including enemy combatants. Golda Meier, then prime minister of Israel, gave this human perspective of war its best expression—reminding us that only soldiers are soldiers, and even these soldiers are human—when she said to the Arab states that Israeli armies had just turned back in 1967, "We can forgive you for killing our children, but we can never forgive you for forcing us to kill your children."

More than thirty years later, George Mitchell included this in his report on the Israeli/Palestinian conflict:

> Palestinians are genuinely angry at the continual growth of settlements and at their daily experiences of humiliation and disruption as a result of Israel's presence in the Palestinian territories. Palestinians see settlers and settlements in their midst not only as violating the spirit of the Oslo process, but also as an application of force in the form of Israel's over-whelming superiority, which sustains and protects settle-ments.

The critical phrase here is "application of force." What does this mean? That Palestinians see the presence of Israeli settlers as it-self an "act"? That the settlers are actively doing something that can be reasonably seen as violent or forceful in a way that im-plies an act of aggression? Which settlers—all? Only the adults? The children too?

If these settlers were living without military companions, these questions would suggest clear answers. The fact that someone lives peaceably in a certain place cannot be seen as a vi-olent act. What, after all, would Palestinians in the Territories say to fellow Palestinians who hold Israeli passports when they move into the neighborhood, beyond "welcome"? The issue here seems to be not the acts of the settlers but their identities. It is not even the fact that they are Israelis (many Palestinians hold Israeli citizenship) but that they are Jews. Thus the presence of the settlers cannot reasonably be seen as "an application of force." But there is more. Along with the settlers come the barbed wire, the tanks and the soldiers standing guard, and the private-access highways, also heavily guarded, for settlers (read Jews) only. Along with the settlers come the military and the enforcement of a two-tiered system of state support and physical infrastructure.

The language in the Mitchell Report seems to speak of how Palestinians see the settlers' presence, but that cannot be separated from the way the Palestinians view the uniformed soldiers, the tanks, and the boundaries and borders and checkpoints that come along with the settlers. So the question here is not so much what it means when a civilian population turns against another civilian population (the Palestinians against the settlers), but what happens when a civilian population turns against the military force that surrounds, and moves alongside, another civilian population. Some small Israeli settlements have no direct military protection, yet even there the settlers enjoy legal rights to carry arms—often supplied by the Israeli government—while Palestinians in the same communities do not.

This example suggests that the individual is implicated by what is done to protect him or her. Am I a soldier? No. Does my presence bring the presence of soldiers too? If so, the innocence of the civilian as a potential target—as the object of war—is uncompromised. But the innocence of the individual as an actor, as one who brings the face of war to others, is not as simple to embrace.

## THE REGULAR AND THE IRREGULAR

One of the most important moral distinctions among people fighting wars is between uniformed soldiers and "irregulars." That word, irregulars, in the past has meant many things, but today it generally refers to people who are actively fighting against an army, police force, or regime with a conscious sense of taking sides and belonging to a larger organized fighting force. Viet Cong guerrillas were irregulars—they generally did not wear uniforms, were often short of arms, and frequently operated outside a chain of command and control, but each knew that he was a part of an organized force and working toward a common military goal. In Afghanistan, the troops of the Northern Alliance were until the beginning of the second great wave of American funds and material irregulars, operating in semi-autonomous units, regularly without uniforms, responding as much to rumors of their leaders' intentions as to orders or plans. Among the first supplies the United States sent the Northern Alliance in 2001 were standard-issue uniforms, in part to help them move toward the status of regular soldiers, and in part so that American soldiers and operatives could tell them apart from their opponents.

John Walker Lindh, referred to in the press as "the American Taliban," was a case study in what it means to be an irregular. He had been a student in a religious school in Pakistan and had seen a number of his fellow students set off, mostly on foot, to become religious fighters in Afghanistan. He followed, reporting along the way to whatever organized groups of self-appointed soldiers he could find. Eventually he wound up a prisoner of Afghan and American forces, and was part of an uprising at the desert castle that served as his prison, along with dozens of other prisoners, some clearly part of organized fighting units and others, like Lindh, not.

Two prisoners managed to get hold of grenades and attacked their keepers. The prisoners were overpowered but made a final stand in the basement—perhaps better called a dungeon—of the ancient castle. The prisoners apparently expected a long fight: they took a horse down with them, for food. The first Americans who ventured into the basement were shot. The insurrection lasted for days, until the Americans decided to flood the dungeon, and many of the prisoners chose to surrender rather than drown.

Among the casualties in those days of battle was an American named John Spahn, a member of the CIA's tactical operations branch. Spahn did not wear a uniform. That, in fact, was one of the tactical advantages of deploying CIA operatives rather than, or in addition to, uniformed soldiers. But Spahn was not an irregular: he was part of a carefully organized and controlled chain of command, acting on orders. As such, he bore the full moral weight that any uniformed soldier must bear. Any soldier is implicated in the larger project of his nation's military by wearing the uniform or taking a clear place in the chain of command: the soldier is an active part of the larger enterprise.

Can we say the same about the irregular? In this case, can we say the same about Lindh? He crossed borders to study and then to fight as part of organized groups that proclaimed their hatred for the United States. These groups also proclaimed their intent to work against the United States, to try to destroy it and its people. Lindh took up arms and understood that he was a fighter in an army against his native country. Clearly, he was a soldier. It is easy to distinguish him from the children who cheered him on as he set off to fight. Those children were not soldiers, however much they might have wanted to be, or even if they believed they were. The old men and women who may have been with him in spirit but sat on the sidelines were not soldiers, even if they wished to be.

But consider, again, the French schoolchildren singing *La Marseillaise*—every child proclaiming himself to be a soldier. Are they the same as Spahn? As Lindh? No, they are not, but to understand in what ways not, we must understand—and agree on—what *La Marseillaise* is really saying. If we are talking about resistance to invading "tyrants," and every man, woman, and child is fighting to repel these unwelcome invaders, then the French combatants have the high moral ground: they are acting as individual agents to defend their homes and families. If they are part of a larger project, it is a defensive one. French children in this hypothetical situation, fighting alongside their parents, would seem to be soldiers only in the very best sense. But would they make fair targets, as a uniformed combatant would? This is an easy question: no. These children are defending their homes against invasion. So long as the invaders are up to immoral work to begin with, these children soldiers are not fair targets. Indeed, no one is a fair target, because the larger project of invasion is immoral.

But there are other considerations here. Is this an unprovoked invasion? What if the invaders are assaulting a civilian population as part of a larger, well-motivated project? Let us say it is the French invading the United States in 1850, to come to the aid of the millions of slaves in the South? Or imagine an invasion force moving in on the home islands of Japan in the 1930s, in response to Japan's cruel imperialism throughout Asia.

In these cases the narrow, individual aspects of home defense are valid, but the larger project is not. The question now becomes, What is my home? My home, literally, is the house I live in. My nation is my home only in a metaphorical sense. I have a right to the quiet enjoyment of my home. What right do I have to my nation, particularly if my nation is up to no good, like enslaving millions of people or invading China? There is no inherent right to the integrity of the nation without regard to that nation's actions. The moral obligation to aid the innocent when attacked will place any state that attacks the innocent, inside or outside its borders, in legitimate peril. When the political actions of the state are justified by "defending the homeland," the game of language has been lost. This is precisely the trick of language employed by countless nations that in time of war take up identities like "The Motherland" (in this case, to borrow the moral cloak of motherhood). Just War thinking must demand a stripping away of moral arguments that cling to metaphor and verbal fancy. Saying things plain is the task.

When Colin Powell was chairman of the Joint Chiefs of Staff during the Gulf War, he had occasion to make a presentation to the assembled press corps about a particularly impressive encampment of Saddam Hussein's Republican Guard. Powell took out a pointer and stepped to a board that held a map of the area in question. Indicating where the Republican Guard was thought to be, Powell said, "What we're going to do is we're going to surround it, cut it off, and kill it." I remembered thinking that his language was more direct—more honest—than most military briefers generally managed. But, on reflection, there was more. Yes, he was blunt about the work of the American military: to kill. But his language stopped short of an even higher measure of decency—recognizing humanity in those we are about to destroy. How much less pleasant it would have been, after all, to hear our general say "We are going to surround them, cut them off, and kill them." And that, in fact, is what we did. Would we have done any differently had Powell's language invested these enemy soldiers, soon to die, with their full measure of humanity? Likely not. Yet the difference in meaning we would attach to the ugly work of our soldiers would have an effect. It would remain in the national conscience as an indication of what war is about. And one can hope it would diminish to at least some degree our appetite for more.

## THE BURDEN OF OUR AGE

Ralph Waldo Emerson famously said that each generation must write its own books. Certainly our generation must write its own Just War theory. Augustine's ideas help in that task. Kant helps. Clausewitz helps. Indeed, all that has come before, all that we may read and think about, helps us choose the ideas we can believe in to justify the most horrible necessary actions of our time. But no earlier age can give us a complete vision of why and when to fight. That we must compose for ourselves.

Today wars and the threat of war thrive as they always have. Perhaps the most remarkable fact about life in the nuclear age is the drive of mankind to survive while continuing to make war. Even after every wise man and woman went on record in the 1950s and 1960s to declare that war must end or else we will destroy our species, war has not stopped and here we still are. The advent of nuclear weapons as well as a range of other technologies, including civilian air travel, the Internet, and the ever-growing infrastructure of global trade, have made the demands of Just War thinking more complex. The spread of electronic media has also meant that the experience of ordinary people in the far corners of the world now has visceral meaning for many who live in the cities and towns of the United States. My children see on the front page of the morning newspaper the images of a Palestinian father trying—and failing—to protect his twelve-year-old son's life while caught in a crossfire between Israeli troops and Palestinian gunmen, and they begin thinking about Just War at an early age, with a fairly complex starting point. Meanwhile, television images of my family—or if not us, then the material world we live in—sit on the television stands of Asia and Africa, the Baltics and the Balkans. American symbols and things, or policies and our people, become real to some small degree in these other worlds. But what meaning do we, our possessions, and our ideas have in the far corners of the world?

The essayist Katha Pollitt takes up this question in her widely discussed essay published shortly after September 11, 2001, "Put Out No Flags." Pollitt, a veteran of the movement against the American war in Vietnam and a longtime activist on the left, faces her daughter upon her return on September 11 from high school, literally across the street from the World Trade Center. Pollitt does not tell her readers what her daughter saw that day, but in all likelihood she witnessed more than her share of horror and managed to return home to her mother to tell about it. Done with her talk, daughter tells mother that they must fly an American flag from their large living room window, because the flag is a symbol of hope and survival. No, her mother says, they will not fly the flag; it is a symbol of war, racism, and imperialism.

Pollitt's domestic compromise is for her daughter to fly the flag from *her* bedroom window, her mother's protests notwithstanding. But mother and daughter do not compromise intellectually or morally. They have no common vocabulary for what America is, and no common understanding of what the American flag symbolizes. It is not too much of an exaggeration to say, further, that in any practical sense they do not agree on what is worth fighting for—and this at a moment when all the wheels of the American will to fight are turning rapidly. Their argument hits a brick wall in Pollitt's essay. It is hardly an argument at all; no agreement, no exchange, no ability to act in concert follows. Pollitt's views are hard and fixed. Her daughter's are fresh and undeniable. Their positions remain poles apart.

This household drama of ideas points to a missed opportunity of enormous proportions. Genuine dialogue and even compassion by both players in this drama are precisely what the American nation needed at that particular moment, in public and in private, in the corridors of power and in every household. Thoughtful protest furthers both.

Pollitt's essay is an intelligent display of opposed beliefs knocking into each other. Hope lies in what might come next, in the synthesis of each generation's position with its opposite. That making of something new, indeed of something better, is the work of protest at its best and forms a rich context for the moral consideration of war, a context of creative thought and openness to the ideas that might emerge to make war unnecessary. If we believe that one purpose of Just War theory is to limit war—rather that merely to justify war—we must see that the best kind of protest presents an opportunity for thought and creativity, a powerful adjunct to the intellectual tools of Just War thinking.

About three weeks after September 11 I made my first trip back to New York, a city I continue to think of as my home.

Like Pollitt I'd been troubled—offended even—by the forest of
flags that sprouted on every clean surface and hung from every
doorway and radio antenna in my suburban Chicago neighborhood. But as I walked south in Manhattan, heading from mid-
town to the site of the attack at the southern tip of the island,
my view of the flag began to change. At about Thirty-fourth
Street the smell of the smoldering World Trade Center site became noticeable. Below West Fourth, the streets were wet. I
imagined that the air itself was being hosed down to keep the
toxic plume of dust and remains to a minimum. Below Canal
Street, about a mile from the Trade Center, shop and ware-
house windows were broken and blown out. Cranes to the
south were loading twisted steel onto river barges. Odd bits of
debris drew attention—shop doors that would not close, bits of
paper and cloth on the wet street. Just behind one particular
shattered window in an old brick building on the second or
third floor, a large, dirty American flag hung. Seeing it, I was
struck by its meaning. It did not represent an easy gesture, an
act of shallow patriotism or conformity, but was instead a statement of endurance. Its meaning had changed profoundly for
me.

All symbols, of course, can change. Meaning is poured into
them just as meaning pours out. This is the lesson of Pollitt's
essay for me—an unintended one, I think, but an important
one, a lesson that helps answer the question, What do images of
America and Americans mean to those distant places who don't
know us but see us in fragments of images and symbols? The
meaning of America to the rest of the world, just like the meaning of the American flag to Americans, is a dynamic thing. Others in the world may see us as warriors, as capitalists, as the rich
and the strong out to take advantage of the weak. They may see

us as Christian Crusaders. Or they may see us as keepers of ideas that liberate and celebrate the individual. Or they may see us in one of a hundred variations on these and other themes. The choice is very much ours, and the best action we can take is to show the world our protesters as well as our warriors, our doubts as well as our certainties, our questions as well as our answers.

# 7

# A JUST WAR THEORY FOR THE TWENTY-FIRST CENTURY

GIVEN ALL THAT WE HAVE SEEN in our age and what we know of what has come before, what platform for Just War thinking still stands and seems relevant in our world today? And what might we add to it, to enable us to think and judge questions of war now—of the wars our leaders contemplate on our behalf?

## WE MUST REAFFIRM THE PRINCIPLE OF NONCOMBATANT IMMUNITY

Catholic Just War doctrine, such as it is, offers a vocabulary of inquiry that is certainly worth preserving. We benefit greatly from asking whether war can be fought in a way that minimizes harm to civilians. Hidden in this question is a church notion called "double effect," a response to ever-recurring impulses to take the pacifist teachings of Jesus at face value. Yes, says the church, killing *is* wrong, and the killing of innocents is even more wrong than the killing of an armed combatant. But when we kill, we might do more than kill. We might protect as well. When the errant bomb falls by accident on the civilian house, we are indeed doing wrong, but we are doing right, too, if that bomb had meant to fall on the weapons and war machinery of the evil. Thus "double effect": the *jus in bello* version of "discrimination." On it hinges the very prospect of Just War. We know that war is wrong. We must believe that in some ways, to an even greater degree, war is also right if we are ever to believe that we are decent people, even though our armies are active throughout the world.

## WE MUST REAFFIRM THE QUESTION OF LEGITIMATE AUTHORITY

Other criteria of Catholic Just War doctrine also are well worth preserving. One of them is whether a war is being led by a legitimate authority. This is not an easy question—legitimacy is a complicated idea when applied to the notion of authority in time of war. Yet it is vital as we seek to understand who exactly is choosing to make war and what the status of the individual soldier is. Is this armed combatant part of a system he supports, if not by supporting the leader of the moment then by supporting the system that has brought that leader to power? Or is this soldier closer to a prisoner, as the soldiers of Adolf Hitler and Saddam Hussein seem to have been? Are the aims of the authority waging this war so base that even if popularly supported they rule out any decent sense of legitimacy? Catholic Just War doctrine will not answer these questions for us, but it does rightly insist that they be asked.

## LAST RESORT?

The Catholic Just War principle of last resort is pointedly not among the criteria that I suggest we reaffirm. Yes, war should be avoided, yet as Michael Walzer and, more recently, Joy Gordon have written with specific reference to the Gulf War and Iraq, what nations do instead of war—blockades, propaganda campaigns, and restrictions on trade—often create terrible harm for the weakest among an enemy nation's civilians while leaving the military and political leadership intact. Thus they enact precisely the reverse of the discrimination principle. Particularly in a military dictatorship, scarce resources tend to concentrate among those with power. To limit trade in fuel, food, and any of the building blocks of civic life is to impose a greater burden on the innocent when we understand that the ruling class will take its share, and more, first.

## LIKELIHOOD OF SUCCESS?

The Catholic Just War principle of likelihood of success is also not here, because that principle too easily serves the interest of entrenched power more than the interests of a general civilian population. In almost all cases, an incumbent government, no matter how unjust, has a greater chance for success than an insurgent force. Neville Chamberlain saw too little likelihood of success in resisting Hitler; those who would have opposed the American South to put an end to slavery saw too little likelihood of success to intercede. By what reasonable standards would the American colonists have predicted success against the British? Or, for that matter, what degree of reasonable success would the early Christians have been able to predict in their resistance to the official restrictions of the Roman Empire? Of course, the early Christians were not fighting a war. They were believers in a vision of the world that required and rewarded total devotion beyond the calculations of probable success. Yet many with the same degree of passion take up arms—consider the American revolutionaries, the African National Congress in apartheid South Africa, the Jewish Brigade of His Majesty's Army in the Second World War, or the simple patriot of the typical small nation, ready to fight to repel any would-be invader. In some ways the criterion of likelihood of success seems to say to the soldier of the lost cause, Save your passion for church; give to the army only the dispassionate commitment that is bound by reason.

At its best, the criterion of likelihood of success holds armies back from destructive conflict that would likely have no good ends. Yet it seems to rob the act of war of its highest claim to necessity: to do what is right, what is morally imperative, what can be accomplished by no other means. Thus it becomes, indirectly, a kind of self-canceling argument: fight only when you can win. But in the background sits the idea that one must fight only when there is no other option. The likelihood-of-success principle seems predicated on the idea that not fighting is always an option. So if this principle is valid, why fight at all? Why not always choose peace? The only answer must be that not to fight, and thus to let the worst happen, is morally unacceptable—that war is just only when the motive is so decent that to have fought the good fight and lost is preferable to have sat out and been spared. All this is really a variation on George Bernard

Shaw's anti-church question, What price salvation? If war *can* be just, but still rare and undertaken only to preserve the highest good, likelihood of success seems an impossible criterion to consider.

## WE MUST REAFFIRM THE IDEA OF
## SAFE PASSAGE AND DUTY TO THE ENVIRONMENT

From Jewish Just War teachings we ought to take the principle of concern for civilian populations (in particular, the biblical injunction to provide civilians safe passage out when laying siege to a city) and a distinct regard for preserving the environment in times of war (in stark contrast to Saddam Hussein's torching of Kuwaiti oil wells at the close of the Gulf War). These two practical challenges are especially important given the state of our world today, and present serious challenges to a power like the United States that often wages war from the sky, too far removed from the sites of destruction to protect civilians effectively.

The failed strategy of "safe havens" during the war in Bosnia is a vivid illustration of the insufficiency of good intent in seeking safe passage for civilians, but that does not argue against its importance. The question of a war-making state's responsibility for the civilians caught up in its killing is among the most difficult for states that act from genuinely good motives yet nonetheless do terrible harm to civilian populations.

Kant's emphasis on the fitness of combatants to resume their roles as citizens following a war's end is relevant here: the armed force that has treated civilians well while ousting their government, and has offered them clear and practical means of escape from areas of battle, will be a far more credible force in administering the peace that follows. (The test of this very principle is unfolding in the aftermath of the second American war against Iraq.)

Taking account of environmental damage in war is especially vital in our era of environmental change. Not only ought any army seek to avoid the macro-environmental effects of poisoning long-term natural resources, but the pervasive use of land mines stands as a measure of long-lasting environmental horror on a small scale, replicated millions of times on every continent except North America.

## WE MUST REAFFIRM THE SANCTITY OF ALL HUMAN LIFE

The traditional religious teachings of Judaism and Islam share a quite specific principle of the sanctity of all human life. To save one life, both traditions teach, is to save all mankind. Small acts of decency are redemptive in both traditions, and the lesson for the soldier is to preserve a personal sense of honor and goodness even while serving in the larger enterprise of war. The Quran returns many times to the idea that wars can be justified not only in self-defense but also to defend innocent third parties who have been attacked or dispossessed. The Islamic laws of highway robbery are also vital: their concern for preserving the common good and the regular workings of public life, particularly public trade, and making and keeping the public sphere safe, absolutely condemn the kind of terrorism that aims to destroy the public life and sense of safety of any civilization.

## WE MUST RESPECT THE PERSONAL
## EXPERIENCES OF WAR

From traditional tribal views of war, we are well advised to take the notion that individuals reveal and shape their own moral natures in war. More specifically, we ought to take the idea that one's actions in war create who one is. Some feel that any bad act is pardonable in war. To the contrary, tribal cultures thought that any act in war carried special meaning, and that idea is worth embracing today. At its far limit, this notion can lead to a craving for war, which is of course a bad craving but an understandable one. To create a culture that does not require—and therefore create—war, the cultural task of transferring what is good about war to acts of peace is imperative. William James is only one of a long line of thinkers and writers to take up the task of imagining how to offer young men and women the danger, self-sacrifice, and public stage that war provides, but without the task of killing and dying. Still, community service will never replace war as a crucible for the soul, because the stakes remain small compared to the epic stakes of war. Fisticuffs or warlike lawyering or salesmanship or the pursuit of any otherwise peaceful occupation in a martial manner might scratch that itch, but toward what end? The self-serving quality of mock battle defeats its own purpose. Even moments of real heroism, the small or large acts of self-sacrifice that involve genuine risk and serve the common good, tend to occur when the world is not watching; they are not part of the drama of national character and purpose that war brings with it. The families of American victims of terrorism abroad, of children killed in the bombing in Oklahoma City, of fallen police and firemen who died on dates other than September 11, of soldiers killed in training maneuvers—these families ask why their losses are not as noteworthy as the losses of men, women, and children in the World Trade Center. Why the hundreds of millions of dollars in relief for the families of the Trade Center victims and not for families of others? All this is largely a matter of the stage of war, of the declaration of a larger story that stops us all in our tracks, puts us all at risk to some small degree, and touches all our lives at least in some small practical way. Of course, no one deserves the tragedy of being at the center of such things. But from another perspective, everyone does—everyone who makes a sacrifice, who is ready to give his or her all—deserves for the moment of that sacrifice to be infused with collective and communal meaning and for the world to take note. Certainly the rush of volunteers to the Trade Center site tells this story to a degree, as does the rush by millions of Americans to give blood—though in fact there was little need for it, and much of the blood collected from donors in the weeks following September 11 was later discarded. The tribal idea of war as a natural event in which every man would participate gave a role in the shared drama to every man. We still crave that, and to an extent we still owe it to all those who sacrifice on behalf of the nation. We are well advised to give as many young people as possible some sense of that importance and continuity in their lives.

One of the tragic mistakes in the prosecution of the war in Vietnam was to forget this. Thus soldiers rotated in and out of their units and might find themselves leaving units still in combat to make their way back to an air base, onto a jet, and then back onto American soil within a matter of days, and without fanfare. The idea was to "normalize" the war and spare the country from the deep collective sacrifices that most adults in positions of authority at the time remembered from the Second World War. Thus civilians, who pursued their lives routinely at home, were spared the feeling of personal involvement in the far-off war, and soldiers who returned were without the feeling that most Americans cared much about their lives in Vietnam. Where combat soldiers in the Second World War had weeks or months after their victory to assemble and wait for ships to carry them home—weeks and months spent talking, drinking, gambling, walking the towns of Europe as victors, writing letters home, altogether doing relatively little but in the company of others they had fought beside—the Vietnam veteran had none of that. No victory. No weeks of transition between battle and home. No epic journey by boat back across the sea. He was simply sent home, the stage of history and the feeling of connection to the nation at large mostly denied him.

## THE BEDROCK OF MORAL ACTION: THE RIGHTS OF MEN AND WOMEN

From the vibrant philosophical period in Europe beginning with Rousseau and Kant and extending through Hegel and Clausewitz, we take first and foremost the dramatic principle that legitimacy in government dwells entirely in the citizenry. Wars are just not if they serve the interests of empire, not if they serve the monarch, and not if they serve an elite, but only if they serve the interests of the mass of ordinary people within the state. This is the best answer to the vital question, How can a state act morally? By affirming and protecting the rights of the individual in every action, with every policy, at every turn.

This principle may seem to stand apart from the more explicitly religious Just War traditions, but in fact Enlightenment thinking has pervaded and profoundly changed religious—and particularly Catholic—Just War ideas. Thus the new Catholic catechism grounds its discussion of Just War in a definition of peace that comes, unacknowledged, directly from the Rights of Man philosophy of the great period of revolution in Europe: "Peace is not merely the absence of war, and it is not limited to maintaining a balance of powers between adversaries. Peace cannot be attained on earth without safeguarding the goods of persons, free communication among men, respect for the dignity of persons and peoples, and the assiduous practice of fraternity."

## A JUST WAR IS A WAR ABOUT THE FUTURE, NOT ABOUT THE PAST

From the lessons of our own age, we must add that a Just War is not a war over the past, or even over the present, but over the future. The all-too-fitting illustration is Milosevic's speech on the Field of Blackbirds in Kosovo in 1989, as Soviet rule receded. Six hundred years earlier, in 1389, Serbian knights had been defeated in battle by Ottoman soldiers, and for the next five hundred years the Turks ruled over Serbia. In the vacuum created by the fall of the Soviet empire, Milosevic emerged to call for a war of ethnic cleansing to redeem the Serbian people from their half-millennium of dominance by Muslims. One million Serbs came to hear his speech in 1989. He told them that "once, the Serbian people were brave and dignified," and that the time was coming for them to take up arms to reclaim what they had lost six hundred years earlier.

The claim-to-the-land argument of, first, the Zionists and now the children and grandchildren of displaced Palestinians is another important illustration of this point. In all three examples we see all too vivid expositions of the harm that comes from fighting to avenge past wrongs. War to express rage over the past tends to destroy the integrity and even the very homes of the war-makers, as modern-day Serbians, Palestinians, and Israelis can attest. Inevitably these wars violate the principles of decency called for in every faith tradition and create new atrocities that future generations will themselves seek to avenge.

In this context the idea of Zionism is important to distinguish from the religiously driven commitment to replace Palestinians with Jews in the Occupied Territories. The Zionist movement that led to the establishment of the state of Israel was born in the mid 1800s as a secular movement. Its aim was to purchase enough land in what was then Ottoman Palestine for Jewish communities to grow as self-sufficient communes that would welcome other Jews. In Zionist thinking there was little concern for the Arab people already living there, and no notion of forcefully displacing Arab homes or villages. The legal purchase of land was the immediate tool for making physical space for new Jewish homes and communities. This early Zionist vision was utopian; it was a dream of an impossible ideal future, nonetheless it had the virtue of a forward-looking passion. Yes, nineteenth-century Zionism turned to Palestine because it was the historical home of the Jews described in the Hebrew Bible, but there was little sense of entitlement in Zionist philosophy. Instead it was built on a sense of opportunity and a commitment to create new, democratic forms of government that would ensure individual rights. In 1967, when the Israeli public was debating the future of the lands near Jerusalem recently captured in battle with Jordan, the Israeli philosopher Yeshayahu Liebowitz remarked that the administration of the captured territory and its captive population "will rot the soul of Israel." In the years that followed 1967 and the occupation of that land by Israel, the "settlement" movement emerged and declared its intention to populate the territories with Jewish homes. Some settlers talk of driving the Palestinians there— many in refugee camps since 1948—out of the territories entirely because this is sacred Jewish land. Thus the forward-looking Zionist spirit has in corners of Israel decayed into a backward-looking claim that the land of the Jews two thousand years ago can belong to no one but Jews today. A political vision dedicated to the future has been hobbled by a movement intent on dragging the nation back to its ancient past to settle grudges begun in the Hebrew Bible.

The nation that says, in effect, "We are fighting to be free of domination that we can point to—the tanks in our streets, the soldiers entering our homes," is fighting for the future. The nation that says, "We are fighting because of what your grand-parents did to ours" is clearly not. The revolutionary band that says, in effect, "We are fighting to build new institutions, to give voice to citizens in the institutions of their public lives" is fighting for the future. The revolutionary band that says, "We are fighting because we hate the Russians"—or the Americans, or the Jews, or the Arabs, or the Turks, is clearly not. Legiti-mate Just War thinking centers on the nation to be built, not the nation to be defeated.

American schoolchildren often read the Declaration of Inde-pendence as an abstract statement of philosophy. In fact it was in some ways a belated declaration of war, coming as fighting between the colonies and the British Empire was already under way. Yet its articulation of the character of the new state that the revolutionaries were fighting for was so specific and credible that it not only anchored the civic faith of the American combatants but also dismissed the quality of petty grievance that many willing revolutionaries had dragged with them into battle. The revolution became less about taxes, less about the quality and character of colonial governors; to a remarkable degree it became a struggle over the fundamental rights of the individual. With that document ideas entered the dispute between colony and empire vividly, and the brewing war became perhaps the most important war about the future in American history.

## APOLOGETICS VERSUS RESTRAINT

Explicit writing about the ideas of Just War began as a form of apologetics—the age of the first Christian kings was the age in which the Christian Just War tradition began, and there is little question that a large part of its function was to justify the wars of those kings. But the potential of Just War thinking is vastly greater. Today we have the opportunity to embrace the language of Just War thinking as a frame of reference, as a set of genuine questions and challenges; not as apologetics but as a potentially restraining force.

Even if we do our jobs as thinkers and citizens well, Just War thinking offers us no release, no moral armor or absolution. Just War thinking is not a game of forgiveness. It is part of the noble and humbling human attempt to be good, or at least to be as good as we are capable of being.

## LANGUAGE, INNOCENCE, AND THE DESTRUCTION OF WAR

A final, vital criterion for Just War has to do with the integrity of language and the value of each individual life—two inseparable principles. Simply put, we must name what we do honestly and press language to its limits of directness and clarity. We cannot fight a Just War if we call our enemies anything other than human; we cannot fight a Just War if we call civilians anything other than civilians; and we cannot fight a Just War unless we acknowledge that war is the business of death and destruction. This makes war more difficult to fight and less palatable for a civilian population. As it should be.

# 8

# THREE CONCLUDING
# PRINCIPLES

RECALL THAT Kant's philosophy of war revolved around universal values—only the war that one nation would want other nations to wage can be just. Thus wars of empire are not just, because the invader would not, in turn, wish to be invaded, while wars of self-defense are just, because the defender would indeed want other nations to defend themselves and to lend support in the defense of others.

In the case of the American Civil War, if we take Abraham Lincoln at his word and see the conflict as a war against seccession, we are faced with enormous bloodshed for the sake of an abstract ideal—the Union—and we fail the Kantian test: by its actions in invading the South, the North (in Kant's view) declares that were it to secede from the South, no longer wishing to abet the institution of Southern slavery and perhaps even to reassert its role as a home to escaped slaves from the South, the South would be justified in invading the North, to preserve that same ideal of union. But ought we to take Lincoln at his word? Or, more to the point, which words of Lincoln should we use to construct a true picture of Lincoln the war-maker?

His second inaugural address, along with the Gettysburg Address, reveals a man deeply aware that the Civil War was a war about slavery. Yet in 1862 he wrote to *New York Tribune* publisher Horace Greeley in response to Greeley's accusation that Lincoln lacked direction and purpose in his conduct of the war. Lincoln stated his purpose plainly:

> I would save the Union. I would save it the shortest way under the Constitution. The sooner the national authority can be restored, the nearer the Union will be "the Union as it was." If there be those who would not save the Union, unless they could at the same time *save* slavery, I do not agree with them. If there be those who would not save the Union unless they could at the same time *destroy* slavery, I do not agree with them. My paramount object in this struggle *is* to save the Union, and is *not* either to save or to destroy slavery. If I could save the Union without freeing *any* slave I would do it; and if I could save it by freeing some and leaving others alone I would also do that. What I do about slavery, and the colored race, I do because I believe it helps to save the Union; and what I forbear, I forbear because I do *not* believe it would help to save the Union.

Perhaps we are trapped by the fact that leaders of war are, generally, also leaders of political institutions, and as politicians they often manage to hold mutually exclusive positions, one offered here to a first constituency, and another offered elsewhere to another. (Indeed, Lincoln concluded his letter by writing, "I have here stated my purpose according to my view of *official* duty; and I intend no modification of my oft-expressed *personal* wish that all men everywhere could be free.") Nevertheless, Lincoln would have failed Kant's test. He put the political objectives of union above the moral objectives of freedom and justice. By doing so, he sacrificed any claim to the moral clarity of Kant's views of war, and of the Just War tradition at its best.

Vaclav Havel, the president of Czechoslovakia as that nation emerged from decades of Soviet subjugation, stands as an interesting counterpoint to Lincoln. In 1977, Havel, then a playwright and intellectual with no experience in politics, helped publish Charter 77, a document rejecting the domination of the Soviets and demanding individual rights. In 1989 the Charter 77 movement seized the opportunity as the Soviet Union loosened its grip on its client states, and reconstituted itself as the Civic Forum. A month later Havel was elected president. In 1991 the last Soviet troops on Czech soil withdrew eastward, and Czechoslovakia was once again an independent nation, with Vaclav Havel as its president and a man named Vaclav Klaus as prime minister.

Havel addressed the citizenry on January 1, 1991, beginning the tradition of a "state of the republic" speech every New Year's Day. His speech began this way: "Dear fellow citizens, there used to be a time when this country's president could have delivered the same New Year's Address he had given a year before, and nobody would have noticed. Fortunately, that time has passed. Time and history have reentered our lives." Where had time and history been before they reemerged? In the hands of an unelected elite which dictated the course of public policy and public life in Czechoslovakia. Now that power was again in the hands of the citizenry. Havel continued, "By the end of the year at the latest, our parliaments should have adopted three new constitutions—two for the constituent republics and one for the federal state." The new Czechoslovakia would become a federation, not unlike the United States, though instead of thirteen or fifty constituent pieces it would have two: the Czech Lands and Slovakia. Each would have a constitution, as each of the American states has its own state constitution, and the union of the two Czechoslovakian states would be bound by a commonly held national constitution. But this did not happen.

In his New Year's address one year later, Havel was straightforward: "Last year at this time I expressed the hope that we would have a new federal constitution by the end of the year. To be sure, we have had its spiritual, moral, and political pillar—the Charter of Basic Rights and Freedoms—for a year now. But we do not yet have a constitution as such, and it is not even certain that we will have one by June elections, as we promised." In fact the Czechoslovakian people never got their federal constitution. The leader of Slovakia, Vladimir Meciar, embraced the grassroots desire of many Slovakians and declared a new independent state, utterly unconnected to the Czech Lands that many Slovakians saw as a hotbed of cosmopolitan Jews who would inevitably take more than they gave to the rural Christian Slovak people.

Havel's partner in governance, Czechoslovak prime minister Vaclav Klaus, felt that the Czech Lands would be better off without the more rural and less sophisticated people of Slovakia. Havel was against dissolution of the union but chose not to resist. And so the "Velvet Divorce" came to pass, and the two new nations of the Czech Republic and Slovakia emerged. Other post-Soviet nations—the former Yugoslavia was an extreme example, and close at hand—chose different paths, closer to the path of Lincoln. But Havel and his colleagues waved to their erstwhile countrymen, and the separation of the two nations was done. Today Slovakia struggles to reach the economic vitality of the Czech Republic, and its public institutions are markedly less democratic.

How many deaths would have been a reasonable price to pay to keep the two states together as a nation? Given the example of the United States, how long a period of postwar suffering would have been a reasonable price to pay for preservation of the Czechoslovak union?

What motivated Havel and his colleagues as the Velvet Divorce unfolded? Consider a comment by Havel in his 1992 New Year's address: "The causes of the burdensome situation in which we now find ourselves . . . spring from the fact that history has placed before us an unprecedented task: to find ourselves anew." Part of the task of the Czechoslovak nation to find itself was to write its constitution, a task it did not complete. Slovakia did not in fact shatter a national union; it avoided one. Its separation from the Czech Lands was perhaps less similar to the seccession of the American South than it might have been had the Southern states withdrawn from the American constitutional convention, a prospect that was only narrowly avoided by the Northern states' delegates' compromise of principle over the issue of slavery, which Jefferson and many others had wanted the Constitution to prohibit.

Had the Southern states separated then, would a war as bloody have ensued? Perhaps not. In fact, it is not at all unreasonable to see the Civil War as a result of the Northern delegates' compromise on slavery, and the cost in lives as a price paid for the short-term gains of realpolitik. Yet the game of historical "what if" is hard to play. With two weaker countries in America, would Britain, or France, or Spain—or some combination of the three—have reclaimed dominion on the continent? We cannot know. But in 1993, Vaclav Havel, in his New Year's address, offered a glimpse into the moral vision that helped him to steer a course around prospective war and to a lasting peace without bloodshed in his nation:

> We must definitively part with the beliefs that a small coun-
> try like our own should not concern itself with the big affairs
> of this world, because the world is in the hands of the great
> powers anyway; that there is no point in defending our-
> selves, because we will always be overpowered; and, that car-
> ing about the fate of freedom in other parts of the world is a
> luxury that we cannot afford. I should like to repeat that
> joining NATO does not mean merely stepping under a pro-
> tective umbrella held by others above our heads. It also
> means a substantial commitment, an act of recognition of
> our co-responsibility for the cause of freedom and democ-
> racy and of our readiness to make sacrifices in their defense
> in the event of an extremity.

Motivated by the practical desire to join NATO, Havel never-theless makes a strong argument for the kind of broad moral vi-sion that Kant thought the only hope for thinking people and democratic nations—indeed, the only real point of Kant's own metaphysical project of seeking to understand man's purpose. Connection to the larger moral engagements of the world brings peace, and justifies war in the few cases in which war can be justified, and Havel here embraces Kant's notion. Small na-tions have large moral responsibilities, and Czechoslovakia's striking example in its Velvet Divorce—again, in such sharp dis-tinction to the disintegration of Yugoslavia—serves that duty powerfully, not in terms of arms or other material forces but in the realm of ideas. It demonstrates to the rest of the world what is possible, what careful thought and moral reflection can yield in the matters of nations and men.

Yet this is not at all as simple as valuing peace above war. Peace is not in and of itself the highest good; rather, it is a *just* peace— a concept as difficult to define as Just War—that is the highest good. Is this statement a needless repetition? "Just," after all, is a variation on "good," and so to say that peace is not the highest good, but that just peace is, is not far from saying that "good" peace is good while bad peace is not. But there is something substantial here as well. Martin Luther King, Jr.'s writings from prison in 1963 about the violence on the streets of Birmingham, Alabama, during a particularly intense run of civil rights demonstrations and violent police repression, offer some insight: "Over the past few years I have consistently preached that nonviolence demands that the means we use must be as pure as the ends we seek. I have tried to make clear that it is wrong to use immoral means to attain moral ends. But now I must affirm that it is just as wrong, or even perhaps more so, to use moral means to preserve immoral ends." Apply this principle and you may conclude that peace—the most moral of moral means—can be an awful alternative to war if the peace in question enforces immoral ends. King also wrote in the same document, his "Letter from Birmingham Jail": "I have almost reached the regrettable conclusion that the Negro's greatest stumbling block in his stride toward freedom is not the White Citizens Counciler or the Ku Klux Klanner, but the white moderate, who is more devoted to 'order' than to justice; who prefers a negative peace which is the absence of tension to a positive peace which is the presence of justice. . . ." Justice,

King tells us, is sometimes ugly and sometimes even violent in its coming to be.

Can King help us draw lessons from the comparison of the American Civil War with the Velvet Divorce of Czechoslovakia? Without a doubt. His focus on the experience of the individual stands as a remarkable rebuke to Lincoln's emphasis on the abstract ideal of union, and clarifies the wisdom of Havel in allowing peace to prevail over union. In the case of the Civil War, Lincoln's turning away from the experience of the individual slave leaves him distant from the higher moral ground. In the case of the Velvet Divorce, Havel's personal revulsion to the notion of calling men and women—in a small nation, his neighbors—to kill and die for the preservation for a state that did not have the will in itself to hold together, leads him to higher ground.

In the end, justice exists not in the abstract but only in the lives of individuals. Again, look at King's Letter as he describes the difference in his view between a just law and an unjust law: "An unjust law is a code that a numerical or power majority group compels a minority group to obey but does not make binding on itself." This is entirely about the experience of the individual and forces readers to consider the status and identity of individuals. Is *this* individual part of the majority group or the minority? How about *that* individual? With this test of just law in mind, we cannot look at the world without looking closely at each individual. Yet modern war tends to begin not among individuals—not as one individual or group of individuals encounters another, and decides to fight—but among abstractions. Empire is built on the abstractions of nationalism and national identity: England, Holland, or Spain were ideas that one could fight for, but to fight for those ideas was also practical in material ways: the spoils of empire were at stake. This conflation of the abstract and the material in the beginnings of the age of empire was remarkable: it ennobled the base motives of material gain with the pieties of nationalism, and it gilded those pieties with riches. Yet moral judgment is the work of the individual conscience, just as the larger fact of war is entirely the product of many small acts made by individual actors. Following King's lead, we must look to the experience of individuals to see with any moral clarity. Take, for example, the morally conflicted case of the Palestinians.

Which individuals benefit from fighting for Palestinian identity? Which individuals suffer for lack of that identity? Some answers come to mind: displaced residents of homes and communities in Israel; people under military occupation in the Territories. Often, the very same people find themselves in both categories. These fundamental questions of identity have distinct and direct answers—who will benefit? *Him*, and *her*, and *him*—mostly civilians, children, noncombatants. But we must be clear in evaluating the moral worth of Palestinian identity and, more to the point, the fight for that identity. It is just only to the degree that it materially helps these people—and not the plutocrats of movements and causes—and only when that material good is more than a redistribution of suffering (shifting it from Palestinians to Israelis, or from some Palestinians to others). The fight is only just if it results in a net reduction in suffering, of fewer people suffering, and suffering less.

## A CASE STUDY: A WAR THAT ENDURES

Another vivid example of the abstractions of ethnic and religious identity struggling against the will and interests of individuals is the case in India and Pakistan. In 1947 one chapter in the inevitable end of the British Empire played out in South Asia. In that year India gained its independence from Britain, and it split in two (or three, depending on how one counts). The Hindu majority remained in control of the largest part of India as well as the nation's traditional governing institutions, while the Muslim minority gained its own nation in two widely separate pieces.

The region of Kashmir sits between India and the larger of those two breakaway territories, Pakistan. Its mountains are some of the highest, most beautiful, and most dangerous in the world. Kashmir has long had a Muslim majority, though for centuries its Hindu minority, in close alignment with the British during the Raj, has dominated the area. In 1930 a Muslim crowd was fired upon in the capital city of Kashmir by Hindu police, killing twenty-one people. This lit a flame of Muslim anger against the maharaja, a puppet of the British. In 1932 the son of a Kashmiri shawl maker named Abdullah founded the Muslim Conference, the first organized political force in Kashmir dedicated to the interests of the Muslim people there. Abdullah became a friend and ally of Jawaharlal Nehru, the political protégé of Mahatma Gandhi and the head of the Indian Congress party. They shared (loosely) a vision of an independent, socialist India as well as a common hatred of the Hindu landlords of Kashmir. Nehru's ancestors had come from Kashmir, and some say that he was in fact a crypto Muslim.

189

That identity would have made little difference to Nehru, given his unrelenting rejection of religious identity of all kinds. He saw religious identity as the principle cause of division within India and the major obstacle to India's quest to become a modern and peaceful nation. Every policy Nehru enacted as India's first post-Raj prime minister attempted to push India out of its religiously divided past and into a secular socialist future. He was horrified by the awful bloodshed of religious mobs as India gained its independence, and saw the emergence of the separate Muslim state of Pakistan as a great national tragedy. Abdullah was less concerned and sympathized with the dream of a Muslim homeland. He saw Nehru's resistance to Pakistan at least in part as Hindu wistfulness for a fading dominance over Muslim people and land.

The southern end of Kashmir held a Hindu majority, and at the time of partition, Hindus rioted against the Muslim minority there. Sikh refugees forced out of the new emerging state of Pakistan had endured their own suffering at the hands of Muslims and joined in attacks against Kashmiri Muslims that killed tens of thousands. As news of these massacres spread to the north, tribal Muslims from Pakistan poured into southern Kashmir and routed the maharaja's police force. The Indian army arrived, and with it a year of steady fighting. The eventual cease-fire left Pakistan with one-third of Kashmir and India with the rest. Abdullah became the leader of Indian Kashmir, with Nehru's support. Nehru then proposed a UN-sponsored vote to determine the future of Kashmir, certain that Abdullah's support would mean victory for Indian reunification. Abdullah lent Nehru that support in part because he saw such a vote as a wedge that might eventually lead to total independence for Kashmir. But the UN proved unable or unwilling to support the vote, and Abdullah eventually approached the U.S. ambassador to the United Nations, Adlai Stevenson, to seek his support for Kashmiri independence, forever hardening Nehru's position in favor of a single secular India including all of Kashmir. Stevenson did nothing for Kashmir, and over the years India and Pakistan have fallen into a routine of regular military skirmishes and artillery bombardment in Kashmir, neither side gaining an advantage and neither ceding an inch to the other.

Violent conflict between Muslims and Hindus has continued to reassert itself every few years throughout India, where 100 million Muslims still live among close to 900 million Hindus. In the 1980s thousands of Muslims were killed in the Indian region of Assam by Hindu mobs, and large numbers of the remaining Muslim population migrated to Kashmir to seek the safety—real or imagined—of its Muslim majority. At the same time the United States was pouring billions of dollars into Pakistan to support—some argue to create—the extremist Muslim movement that opposed the Soviet Union in Afghanistan (Osama bin Laden among them). As the new Kashmiri refugees resettled, some of that American money made its way to Kashmir to support radical Islamic schools. The children educated in these schools ten and twenty years ago today form the backbone of the Muslim extremist movement in Kashmir as the war continues there between India and Pakistan.

In this history there is a complex interaction between Nehru's vision of a secular democratic socialist state and the vision of an independent Kashmir held by Abdullah and others. Had Nehru's vision taken hold elsewhere in India—had there been no massacres of Muslims by Indian Hindus in Assam, for example—the prospects of a plebiscite in Kashmir, and of a will to remain within the larger state of India, would have been much greater. Yet that did not happen. Nehru's vision was a noble but a failed one. And it hardly seems right to impose the unfulfilled promise of a noble civic failure upon a civilian population that truly believes in another vision, however crude, that serves its collective interest. It is hard to say to the people of Kashmir, You must go Nehru's way because it is a better, more modern way. Yet this is precisely what Nehru, and those who have followed him in India, have said. And the results have been the continuation of fighting between Pakistan and India, and periodic explosions of the will-to-destroy on both sides, to the point that many observers believe nuclear war is more likely over the largely empty high peaks of Kashmir than over any other spot on earth. India will not let go its claims; Pakistan will not let go its claims; and the citizens of Kashmir are largely not consulted but rather conscripted into the armies that face each other over their land.

The troubled heart of the issue here is clear: the self-determination of peoples, the consent of the governed. If a clearly distinct population opposes the rule of a different group over their home territory, the government that rules them by force is not legitimate. It seems obvious that the Muslims of Kashmir, now in large part ruled by the Hindus of India, ought to be allowed to go their own way. Yet it seems almost tragic to step backward from Nehru's modern, democratic, multicultural vision into tribal ethnic territoriality. Is Nehru's vision not worth preserving? After all, the consent of the governed can all too easily become the rule of the mob.

## THREE PRINCIPLES

The challenge of the Indian/Pakistani conflict, as well as the larger question of Just War, becomes easier to engage with three principles in mind:

*First,* that a Just War sanctifies human life and treats all life as equally precious.

*Second,* that a Just War is a war about the future, not the past.

*Third,* that a Just War preserves and strengthens the principles of individual rights, based on the notion that the legitimacy of government derives from the consent of the governed.

These principles suggest a clear answer to the question of Kashmir: Nehru's ideal of a state somehow above religious separatism is not worth the forced yoking of a Muslim region to a de facto Hindu state, simply to demonstrate Nehru's point or fulfill his vision. The jealousy to hold territory, on the part of both nations, is insignificant to the core of Just War thinking. Arbitrary national borders do not enter into the question of right governance, as they do not enter into the question of Just War. The will of the people and the recognition of the value of each and every life among them is the pillar upon which any lasting and decent solution must stand. If the people of Kashmir wish independence, even for reasons others may regard as wrong or less evolved, their will must trump the theories of others.

To reject this notion in Kashmir is to hold too little respect for the lives lost and distorted by the fight to keep Kashmir attached to India (and thus it does not sanctify human life. After all, no one argues that Kashmir must be kept Indian to save the lives of Kashmiris, not even India). To reject this notion is to look backward—among the intelligentsia, to the fleeting image of a united post-British India as imagined by Nehru; among far too many Indians in the streets, to the bloodbath of Pakistan's separation. Neither Pakistan nor India have asked the people who live in Kashmir to decide their own fate.

The first question of the Just War tradition has long been, Is this war being led by a legitimate authority? Until the people of Kashmir control their own government, no war fought over Kashmir (and for the past half-century, war over Kashmir has meant war *in* Kashmir), save perhaps a war of independence, can be just. And with this observation we note an historic shift, a dramatic modernization of Just War thinking. It is the shift from the *question* of legitimate authority, redolent with ambiguity in the ancient beginnings of Just War thinking, to the *affirmation* that legitimate government requires the consent of the governed, and that a Just War simply cannot be waged by the agents of a state that holds its citizens captive. In this observation, a unity of the central ideas of Just War thinking begins to emerge: recognition of the equality of men and women—not in their wretchedness but in the sanctity of all human life—underscores the central importance of the consent of the governed. The argument is simple: no ruling class is worthy of governing without the consent of the governed, because no class is of greater inherent worth—or closer to the goodness of God—than the people generally.

This notion of the equal sanctity of all human life is the irreducible center of Just War thinking. It is the assumption we must share in order to have any hope of a more peaceful future or a more decent world. And it is the most obvious missing piece in the worldviews that produce the most awful atrocities.

Indeed, its absence predicts not only terrible violations against enemy populations but a degree of debasement in any aggressor's forces and its own civilian population.

Part of the story of the battle of Kosovo in 1389 is that as Prince Lazar of the Serbs was choosing between surrender and a fight to the death, Elijah appeared to him with a message from the Virgin Mary: "What Kingdom shall I choose?/ Shall I choose a heavenly kingdom?/ Shall I choose an earthly kingdom?/ If I choose an earthly kingdom,/ An earthly kingdom lasts only a little time,/ But a heavenly kingdom will last for eternity/ and its centuries." Similar to Palestinian and Al Qaeda suicide bombers, the Serbian nationalists who recite this poem declare that death is preferable to life, not because others will live while soldiers die, not because the sacrifice of a few is preferable to the sacrifice of the many, but because death is better than life.

Wars by their nature are organized and prosecuted by a leadership class. When that class teaches those who follow them to rush into death because death is itself glorious, they have failed and have sacrificed their legitimacy. Death may be necessary in war but should be minimized. The bravery of the dead may be celebrated, they may be missed and mourned, but if soldiers or citizens are led to love death more than life, something is terribly wrong.

The principle of sanctification of life is also essential in considering the merits of a war's cause or the proportional goodness of its ends. Karl Marx wrote about the American Civil War in 1862, in the German newspaper *Die Presse*, that "Up to now we have witnessed only the first act of the Civil War—the *constitutional* waging of war. The second act, the revolutionary waging of war, is at hand." Abraham Lincoln, Marx correctly observed, had discovered the moral logic of the Civil War as its new purpose, rather than the merely constitutional. Lincoln had first portrayed the essence of the war as the preservation of the nation, but midway through, for a range of reasons we can only speculate upon, his rhetoric moved from the state-engineering notion that a house divided against itself cannot stand to the belated moral clarity of the Emancipation Proclamation. Three years into the war, this document finally gave federal imprimatur to the notion that slavery was wrong. Only then did the Civil War discover its just cause. In this case, one kind of war is in fact better than the other. It is better to end slavery that to tolerate it. It is better to fight for all citizens' right to control and protect their own lives than it is to fight only for political virtue.

The Civil War became a better war when Lincoln found its moral center, just as the Second World War became a better war in the collective American conscience when it shifted from a war against German imperialism to a war against German genocide, a view that began to emerge only as the war was ending and the scale of the Nazi death camps emerged for the world to see. How can these moral distinctions possibly matter when they came only after wars had begun, or were nearly concluded? Because of the next war to be fought, or to be avoided. The national sense of when and why a war can be just was sharpened in both cases, and though the morally elevated versions of each war's story were obviously myths, those myths said much about what our nation wanted to be, and could become, if we were to hold tightly enough to the moral principles we were enshrining ex post facto.

The late discovery of the moral high ground in the Second World War made a great deal of difference in Bosnia. The new sense of the Civil War made a great deal of difference—though, tragically, a full hundred years later—for the civil rights movement in the decade from 1955 to 1965. In both cases, the emergence of the equal sanctity of all human life as a central value in the moral perspective on these wars came to matter a great deal as the nation took up later struggles.

A personal test of this idea came to me over a conference table at Harvard University where I was teaching the course Moral Principles of War. A student challenged my proposition that respect for life was a higher good than national sovereignty. In that case, he said, I'd be forced to support an invasion of the United States, by, as an example, France in 1830 if their invasion sought to free the American slaves. Well, of course I would have to support that, I replied, and I assumed that everyone around the table would as well. Yet few agreed with me, though I still hold this opinion firmly. I consider the perspective of the slave, contemplating the misery of bondage and asking, Who will save us? Almost any answer to that question bestows some virtue on the savior.

Is war for an ideal, or even for a political outcome, worth the spilling of blood? If we begin with the notion that war is justified only when it saves lives in the long run, or preserves and extends human freedom in the most dramatic ways (freeing the slaves, for example, may or may not result in a net savings of lives but is an essential act of human freedom), we must reject wars that kill for the sake of concepts like union, national dignity, or—recall Henry Kissinger's comments in the last days of the Vietnam War—geopolitical credibility.

This, finally, is where Just War thinking leads us. In this age we can extend Clausewitz's observation that war is politics by other means to say, as well, that there is no such thing as a Just

War that seeks only political objectives. The three enduring principles of Just War, encapsulating and extending the two-thousand-year-old tradition of Just War thinking, are that a Just War sanctifies human life and treats all life as equally precious; that a Just War is a war about the future, not the past; and that a Just War preserves and strengthens the principles of the rights of the individual, based on the notion that the legitimacy of government derives from the consent of the governed.

These principles do not hold the magic to discern between the time to fight and the time to hold back in any particular case. But they do challenge us to think within a moral framework that holds the value of the individual higher than any abstraction. If we can do that, we will embody that noblest act, the act of human progress.

# AFTERWORD:
# ON THE SECOND GULF WAR

TEN DAYS after I sent a near final version of the preceding pages to my publisher, the American war against Iraq began. I arrived home from a business trip, kissed my family, took to the couch, and watched on television as the first bombs fell on Baghdad in the American attempt to "decapitate" the leadership of Iraq—that is, to kill Saddam Hussein and his two sons as they dined in a basement. The two most notable advances in the TV coverage of the bombing of Baghdad since the previous Gulf War were, first, the greater clarity of nighttime video images and, second, the verisimilitude of the concussive shock that my television managed to deliver to me as it broadcast the sonic effects of twenty-first-century bombs and missiles falling in rapid succession upon single targets.

Undertaken without haste; debated, digested, embraced, and renounced for months before it began, this was a different kind of war from the classic rush to arms. But it was not a new kind of war. The debates and delays, the politicking and parliamentary consideration in the run-up to the shooting war itself made it clear that this was a war of choice, entered into as a matter of strategy rather than concrete and immediate self-defense. Wars of choice are familiar things in human history: both the Hebrew Bible and the Quran offer distinct sets of moral strictures for these kinds of wars. And in the Christian tradition, Augustine was clear that war to aid innocent third parties suffering under the heel of tyrants and warmongers would also be just.

Yet all three religious traditions require some degree of established theocratic rule to set the stage for wars of choice. Because, after all, to go out and make war when none exists is no little thing. The ancient Hebrews and medieval Muslims particularly believed that this kind of war ought to happen only when the inner workings of a divinely ordained and approved kingdom were humming along. Only when the inner struggle to get right with the powers above was well enough won, only when the true believers were confident that their own spiritual and civic houses were in good order, would they be ready to take up arms and go out to encourage, at the tips of their swords, others to get right too, or to die resisting. And so I joined many who believed there might be a kernel of justification of this second Gulf War but were badly troubled by the hubris of our leader, calling our nation the repository of all that is good, and our enemy, quite simply, evil. I felt that we as a nation could not be as purely good, and ought not to be as self-satisfied, as our unilateral actions declared we were.

But that is too simple an answer to a large and complex question: Was the second American war against Iraq a Just War by any reasonable standards?

# AFTERWORD: ON THE SECOND GULF WAR

The Bush administration made a number of linked arguments for the war. First, that Saddam was an evil ruler and deserved to be removed on his personal merits. Second, that the terms of the 1991 cease-fire concluding the first Gulf War were being abrogated, and the United Nations was making itself irrelevant to the world by failing to enforce those terms. Third, that Iraq was a rogue nation which had armed itself with weapons of mass destruction and posed an active threat to the world. And fourth, that Iraq had ties to Al Qaeda and bore some responsibility for the September 11 attacks on the United States, and would likely help support future attacks.

Some justification for a war can be based on each of these arguments.

Without question, Saddam Hussein was an abusive ruler who had lost all moral standing to continue in power. His persecution of Iraqi Kurds and of the Sunni minority in Shi'a-majority Iraq, and his fascistic domination of Iraqis of all backgrounds, were more than ample reason to justify a concerted effort by outsiders to push Saddam out, by some degree of military force.

Saddam was indeed making a mockery of the UN and reinforcing the perception among tyrants that the world organization lacked the practical strength—to say nothing of the collective will—to deter future genocidal maniacs.

And the UN inspectors who had been expelled from Iraq had plausible suspicions that Iraq had at various points manufactured and stored chemical and biological weapons, and was attempting to build nuclear weapons. Evidence came from inspectors who had spent months and in some cases years on the ground in Iraq, from Iraqi scientists and military leaders who had defected, and from Iraq's observed history of deploying chemical and biological weapons against civilian populations and against the Iranian army.

Only the last point, about Iraq's alleged ties to Al Qaeda, seemed farfetched and implausible. Saddam had opposed Islamic extremism throughout his public career and had been ruthless in suppressing whatever sparks of Mujahideen culture had appeared in his nation. Only a common hatred of the United States linked Saddam and bin Laden.

Even if the Bush administration was correct in three of these four allegations, though, were they enough to justify war? The Catholic church is quite clear today that preemption of an anticipated military threat does not justify war. And the pope himself called for more negotiation just before the first American and British military attacks on Iraq.

Yet the highest moral ground held by the advocates for war was the Christian ground of defense of the innocent. So we can quickly answer the question of whether some kind of war against Saddam was just—that answer is yes, just as a war against the Nazi leadership of Germany was just, and just as a war against the slaveholding interests of the pre–Civil War American South would have been just—all in the name of coming to the aid of the millions of innocents suffering under the misrule of their own nation's leaders. The most critical question is not whether some kind of war against Saddam was just, but whether *this* war, specifically planned and executed by the Americans with the support of the British and sundry smaller nations, was just.

The answer, in my view, is that the war as fought failed to meet the test. The United States could have—and therefore should have—done better. The traditional Just War criteria of last resort, legitimate authority, and discrimination are all arguable in this case. Yet the more forward-looking criteria of just wars as wars more about the future than the past, wars that sanctify all human life equally, and wars that strengthen the rights of the individual make it clear (at least to me) that we failed in important ways to choose a morally satisfying path, the least objectionable of the generally awful options that faced the United States and the United Nations in 2002 and 2003.

Our greatest failings were not in the shooting war itself but in the aftermath. American troops—and, even more so, British troops—were quite effective in distinguishing civilians from soldiers of various kinds, though with no shortage of sad and ugly exceptions. It was not American soldiers but American policymakers who had the most explaining to do. Specifically, in planning for the war American soldiers appear to have been protected to a greater degree than were the lives of Iraqi civilians. British journalist Jon Swain, based in Iraq throughout the fighting, made the case: "The idea has grown in the American army that a good war is one in which no Americans are injured, and out of this has grown the idea that war does not hurt people at all because Iraqis and Afghans, for example, are seen as subhuman." Even from my couch I could see Swain's overreaching. "Subhuman" is too strong. But certainly the lives of Iraqi civilians were openly less important to American soldiers in the weeks after their initial victory than the ideal of "force protection," that is, the lives of the invading soldiers themselves. Perhaps more important, a grudging sense of vengeance permeated much of the on-the-ground understanding of who the Iraqi people were, and how connected they might be to the Saudis and Egyptians who planned and executed the September 11 attacks. At least for many soldiers and a significant number of their leaders, the war in Iraq had a degree of payback as its apparent justification—and that was flatly wrong. Here again is Jon Swain, reporting for the *Sunday Times* of London: "Take Justin Lehew, a gunnery sergeant from New York who gave a pep talk one morning to his marines, who were guarding a group of pathetic Iraqi prisoners. He told them quite wrongly: 'These are people who destroyed my city. Stay motivated. Do not forget why we are here. Stay motivated. Wave at them. But wave at them with an M16.' My *Sunday Times* colleague Mark Franchetti, embedded with young marines getting their first taste of war, wrote about the tragic consequences of this mind-set after they shot up vehicles carrying civilians trying to escape the city of Nasiriya, killing 12 including a baby girl and a boy."

Further, an ugly degree of profiteering by American corporations seems to have followed immediately upon the military victory, and that did the American war effort no moral good. Instead it clouded the motives of at least some policymakers, connected as they were to the corporations in question.

The final judgment of this war, though, will come years and decades from now, when we can see what has risen to replace the Baathist regime of Saddam Hussein. If that turns out to be a nation that recognizes and protects basic human rights, and a nation that clearly takes its legitimacy from the consent of the governed, this war will have been a good deal more just than skeptics today—myself included—declare it to be. But if that nation resembles the oligarchy of, say, Kuwait today (recall the blatant untruth of the first President Bush's promise to "restore democracy to Kuwait," a nation that has never known democracy and denies most of its residents the basic rights of citizenship), it will have failed to meet the unlikely hope of Bush administration intellectuals that this war might bring the Enlightenment to the Arab people and begin to tip the balance of the Middle East toward representative government. If things in Iraq are no better in ten and twenty years than they are today, in 2003, with a collapsed civic infrastructure, or no better than they are in Afghanistan, with its capital city held in trust by foreign powers and a patchwork of warlords' fiefs throughout the rest of that nation, this second Gulf War will stand as a stark and ugly adventure in imperialism.

That the war in Iraq cannot fully be judged for years to come points to the profound link between Just War and just governance. Classical Just War theory points to this in the question of legitimate authority, but that speaks only to just governance within the nation that *makes* war. The governance of the nation that, in some sense, has war *made to it* gets only glancing attention in the traditional Just War idea of proportionality: that the good to flow from a war must be in proportion to the harm that the war itself will do. This linking of Just War to just governance needs to be more explicit in any twenty-first-century Just War philosophy.

All of which leads to a joke now common in the gathering places of educated Baghdadis. It turns out that a man is having trouble sleeping because his neighbor's dog is barking all night. It is a big, ferocious dog, and the man fears for his children's safety just knowing that the dog lives next door. So one day he slips a bit of a powerful poison into the dog's food, and the dog dies. That night the man and his children sleep well. But the next night he hears a dozen dogs barking, and his children are set upon by a pack of mongrels. All these new dogs, it turned out, had been kept at bay by the constant sound of the big dog, now dead.

I like this joke in part because it captures some of the naive good intentions of the United States in Iraq, and in part because it illustrates the foolishness of trying to solve the problems of a shared community by oneself. For in the final analysis, what made this war easiest to fight for the United States—that this was essentially our show—is exactly what will make more difficult the emergence of an Iraq that shares modern standards of just governance. What we failed most profoundly to do was to model in the war itself the kind of consciousness of the larger world that we now ask the Iraqi people to display. In effect we tell them, You must be democratic; You must build civil relations with other nations; You must allow your citizens to function within the larger context of the world at large. But then our actions say, If you get to the point where you really feel threatened, and you don't like the game of common standards and the often complicated and complicating moral principle of the rights of man, pull out your big guns and impose your will on those who are weaker than you are.

To some extent this was Rousseau's answer: when sensible citizens gather together to form a decent government, those few who dissent from the earnestly good principles of a new order will, in Rousseau's words, be forced to be free. Rousseau's social vision saw first and foremost the natural goodness of man, yet even he tipped his hat to the fundamental contradiction of the well-intended builders of better worlds: the balance of force and freedom. The American military proved brilliant in the war against Iraq as it exercised force. But the morality of the equation will become clear only when we have discovered, over time, what exactly we have forced Iraq to be.

# INDEX

# INDEX

Christians, 116. *See also* Crusaders;
Crusades.
Churchill, Winston, 66
CIA, 158
Cicero, 53, 54, 55, 56, 57, 59, 61, 63, 64,
65, 78, 146
*City of God* (Augustine), 62, 72
Civic Forum, 182
Civil rights movement, 197
Civil War, 30, 31, 83, 84, 180; and civil
rights movement, 197; Marx, 195;
slavery, 181, 184, 196; and Velvet
Divorce, 187
Clausewitz, Carl von, 6, 7, 21, 25, 41,
44, 45, 50, 52, 55, 64, 73, 83, 146,
161, 174, 197; biographical details,
42; and the state, 42, 74, 75; war,
philosophy of, 42
Clinton administration, 90
Clinton, Bill, 144
Colombia, 128, 136
Columbia University, 83
Columbus, Christopher, 80
Conference of Catholic Bishops in
the United States, 76
*Confessions* (Augustine), 62
Constantine, 11, 61, 62, 81
"Contest in America, The" (Mill), 31
Cooper, Duff, 33, 34
*Coronation of Napoleon I, The*, 92
Croats, 86, 90–91
Crotia, 86, 88, 89
Crusaders, 27, 116, 125
Crusades, 115, 124; history of, 115–116
Custer, George Armstrong, 5
Czech Lands, 183, 184

Czech Republic, 149, 150, 183, 184
Czechoslovakia, 32, 33, 34, 35, 39, 182,
183, 184, 185, 187

Daladier, Edouard, 33, 35
Damascus, 116
Dark Ages, 118
David, King, 101
Dayton Accords, 90
Dayton (Ohio), 90
Declaration of Independence, 22,
177
Deuteronomy, Book of, 97, 98
Diomedes, 18
Divine monarchy, 43, 44
Domino Theory, ix
Dresden, viii

East Germany, 47, 150
East Prussia, 47, 52
Eastern Europe, 77, 150
Egypt, 97, 99, 108, 116, 117, 119
Eichmann, Adolf, 70, 71, 72
*Eichmann in Jerusalem* (Arendt), 70,
71
Elijah, 195
Emancipation Proclamation, 196
Emerson, Ralph Waldo, 161
England, 148, 187. *See also* Great
Britain.
Enlightenment, 26, 27, 75, 122,
174–175; and Grotius, 48
Estonia, 88
Europe, 39, 48, 82, 96, 121, 174, 175
European Union, 84
Eusebius, 61

# INDEX

Hitler, Adolf, 12, 32, 33, 34, 35, 39, 78, 87, 167, 168

Hittites, 98, 99

Hivites, 98

Hobbes, Thomas, 54

Holland. *See* Netherlands.

Holocaust, 71

Holy Roman Empire, 73

Homer, 6, 18, 19, 20, 59

Hoy, Pat, viii

Hungary, 70, 86

Hussein, Saddam, 23, 24, 33, 39, 78, 98, 115, 128, 135, 167; Gulf War, 129, 130, 145, 170; Islamic extremism, opposition to, 202; reign of, 131; and Republican Guard, 160; Second Gulf War, 199, 201, 204

Hutus, 154

Hyderabad, 118

Hyman, Sidney, 95

Identity: and ethnic, 189; national, 187, 188; religious, 189, 190

*Iliad* (Homer), 6, 18, 19, 20

India, 107, 148; and Great Britain, independence from, 119, 189; Kashmir, 191, 192, 193, 194; religious identity of, 190

Indian Congress party, 189

Iran, 90, 118, 150; and American hostages, 127–128

Iranian revolution, 114

Iran-Iraq War, 132

Iraq, x, 23, 40, 78, 79, 83, 115, 116, 130, 135, 150, 168, 205; and Al Qaeda, 201, 202; British occupation of, 131;

Second Gulf War, 199, 203; war with, 145, 149, 171; and weapons of mass destruction, 201, 202

Isaiah, 101

Islam, xi, 16, 93, 94, 105, 106, 107, 108, 109, 110, 112, 116, 122; and Ataturk, 123; human life, sanctity of, 171; Jihad, 129; and Mawdudi, 119; origins of, 95, 96; and radicalism, 120; revolutionaries, 119, 120; as violent religion, 125. *See also* various Muslim entries; Shi'ite Muslims; Sunni Muslims.

Ismaili Muslims, 117, 118

Israel, viii, 35, 36, 37, 71, 72, 98, 99, 100, 104, 130, 133, 134, 142, 154, 155, 176, 188; establishment of, 176; and settlement movement, 177

Israeli Defense Forces, viii, 142

Israelis, 37, 156, 176

Italy, 35; and Lausanne Treaty, 121

Ivory Coast, 136

James, William, 18, 19, 30, 31, 32, 172

Japan, 148, 154, 159

Jebusites, 98

Jefferson, Thomas, 49, 53, 54, 55, 75, 122, 124, 184

Jena, 83

Jepson School of Leadership Studies, viii

Jerusalem, 61, 115, 116, 176

Jesus, 11, 109, 167

Jewish Brigade, 169

Jewish Just War: and teachings of, 103, 129, 170

# INDEX

# A NOTE ON THE AUTHOR

Peter Temes is the president of the Antioch New England Graduate School in Keene, New Hampshire. He has taught literature, ethics and leadership studies at Harvard, Columbia, and Antioch universities. Mr. Temes has also written *Against School Reform* and *One School Now* and is the editor of *Teaching Leadership*. He lives with his wife and three children in Fairfield, Connecticut.